To Dad

A poetry boo[k]
been missing fr[om your self]
we hope you enjoy it for
many years to come
With all our Love

Jan and Barry

christmas '01

ESSENTIAL NEW ZEALAND
POEMS

ESSENTIAL NEW ZEALAND
POEMS

SELECTED BY

**LAURIS EDMOND
& BILL SEWELL**

GODWIT

A GODWIT BOOK

published by

Random House New Zealand

18 Poland Road, Glenfield, Auckland, New Zealand

www.randomhouse.co.nz

First published 2001

© 2001 selection and introduction: Bill Sewell and the

Estate of Lauris Edmond; poems as credited on page 254

The moral rights of the authors have been asserted

ISBN 1 86962 087 9

Cover and text design: Inhouse design

Layout: Janet Hunt

Printed in Singapore

CONTENTS

INTRODUCTION It has always been true that in dealing with the dilemmas of ordinary life – the inescapable moral, personal, spiritual, even practical decisions that are constantly to be made - people turn to poetry, spoken, or sung, or read. They look for refreshment, for illumination, insight, pleasure, relief.

WITH THESE WORDS, Lauris Edmond stated her views on the role of poetry when she began work on this anthology in 1998.[1] She was never one to make an unnecessary mystery of poetry. Not that it shouldn't have mystery, but that was not the point. She saw poetry as part of people's everyday experience, something instinctive and essential, something addressing them directly and powerfully – something with immediate impact.

Broadly speaking, the concept of 'immediate impact' was the guiding principle for the two editors of this anthology. For us, immediate impact meant that a poem had to present at least some aspect that made it instantly appealing to the heart and the ear – to be memorable, or have a quality that would make the reader want to go back to it, preferably many times. A full understanding might not come until after several readings. Indeed, it might never come – and that didn't really matter, so long as the reader had engaged quickly with the poem in some way.

Of course, immediate impact might be a matter of atmosphere, as in Brian Turner's 'Madrigal' – or humour, as in Bub Bridger's 'Blatant Resistance'. It might arise out of an aspect of New Zealand history, as in Ruth Dallas's 'Photographs of Pioneer Women', or A.R.D. Fairburn's Depression lament 'Down on my Luck'. But it is just as likely to be a quirky and intriguing title, as in Jenny Bornholdt's 'Instructions for How to Get Ahead of Yourself While the Light Still Shines' or an inventive image, as in James Norcliffe's 'the sportsman drops a goal'; or a striking pattern of repetition, as in Rachel Bush's 'Look Here'; or a free expression of emotion, as in Hone Tuwhare's 'Heemi' or Vivienne Plumb's 'Before the Operation'; or, yes, even a seductive sense of mystery, as in Robin Hyde's 'The Last Ones' or Lauris Edmond's own 'Going to Moscow'.

That was our main guideline. And while neither Lauris nor I would have denied that it is difficult to separate immediate impact from personal taste, one thing

---

1. In mid-1998 Lauris invited a number of poets to submit up to ten poems each for the anthology, but she reserved the right to make the final selections. With each invitation she included a brief statement of the aims of the anthology, from which this quotation is taken.

we were sure of: we would not choose poems that seemed to shut out the reader from the beginning. So we did not consider poems showing some of the more extreme features of post-modernism, such as a multitude of voices, or phrases scattered across the page, as well as poems that rely too much on references outside themselves.

This anthology is compiled for the many avid readers who reach out for a new novel, or biography, or perhaps a work of history – but who less often pick out a book of contemporary New Zealand poems. We hope also that it will find a ready place in the classroom. And so, with these readers in mind (rather than academics, or critics, or even poets themselves), we have included many of the major figures of the last hundred years, from Allen Curnow to Cilla McQueen, from Ursula Bethell to Peter Bland; but we have sometimes made unusual, or possibly surprising, choices from the work of these poets. We also looked for work from writers who are not so well known, but whose work deserves wider recognition.

Although our approach differs from most major anthologies, such as the *Oxford Anthology of New Zealand Poetry in English* of 1996, it does invite immediate comparison with Bill Manhire's *100 New Zealand Poems* (Godwit, 1993). Manhire also aimed at the general reader, and at covering the widest possible range in a limited space; but he included only one poem by each poet. We wanted to include a few more poems by many of our poets, and also to bring the selection up to date – since a lot of significant New Zealand poetry has appeared since 1993.

THE OTHER GUIDELINES for selection were largely the practical ones that all editors face if they are not to let an anthology get out of hand. We decided that, all things being equal, we would choose poems with a clear New Zealand connection – in place, culture or history – ahead of those with exotic settings. But that didn't stop us from including such fine poems as Chris Orsman's 'The Last Tent', about the English polar explorer Robert Falcon Scott in the Antarctic, or Harry Ricketts' 'Albergo Sole', set in Rome, or Iain Sharp's 'Smoke', with a Glasgow background.

Because we wanted to include a wide range of poets within a limited space, we had to restrict the number and length of poems chosen from each poet. No poet is represented by more than four poems, and with one exception (Dinah Hawken's minimal sequence, 'Talking to a Tree Fern') there are no full sequences of poems. It is in fact usually short poems or self-contained sections from longer poems that make the immediate impact we were looking for.

1999 was an extraordinary year in New Zealand poetry. New work appeared, for example, from Elizabeth Smither, Bill Manhire, Alistair Te Ariki Campbell, Michele Leggott, Fiona Farrell, James Brown, Gregory O'Brien, Robert Sullivan, Harvey McQueen and myself. Paola Bilbrough, Emma Neale and Mark Pirie published their first collections. The year 2000 did not really slow the flood, but there had to be a cut-off date for this anthology. And the neatest solution was to make it the end of the old millennium. The editors were, however, reading and considering poems from new volumes right up to the end of November 1999, and poets who published in that year are well represented.

FINALLY, A WORD about the arrangement of the poems. Every system has its drawbacks. An arrangement by subject seemed arbitrary; an arrangement by time creates the problem of whether to list poets by their date of birth, or by the date of their first publication. Also, we were aiming to introduce readers simply to good poems, not to reveal any particular themes, or historical development. In the end we settled for the democratic and easily navigable alphabetical order.

I hope readers will enjoy finding their way around this selection as much as we did – reaching back into New Zealand history, assessing the current state of our poetry, meeting new writers, getting a foretaste of the future, encountering old friends and making surprising discoveries. Anthologies are, of course, always the product of their time, and of compromise. But I believe that this one, arrived at over many readings, discussions and deliberations by two poets of different ages and experience, will offer – for many years to come – a broad and satisfying picture of the achievements and promise of New Zealand poetry at the end of the 20th century.

NOTE

Lauris Edmond invited me to help her compile this anthology in July 1999, and by the end of November 1999 we had produced a draft selection. Then, on 28 January 2000, Lauris died suddenly. Her death was an enormous loss to the project. However, it was clear to me that she had left a solid legacy to continue with: first, her own commitment to the anthology, which her literary executors shared; and, secondly, the draft selection itself, which I realised needed only some fine tuning. I constructed this introduction in large part from correspondence and from my notes and memories of conversations with Lauris about the anthology.

A number of individuals have helped to shape this anthology and bring it to fruition. I would like in particular to acknowledge the assistance of Bridget Williams, Anne French, Ken Arvidson, Harry Ricketts and Frances Edmond. Others, too numerous to list here, also contributed support and advice at various stages, and to them too I owe thanks.

Bill Sewell
Wellington, December 2000

FOR ANDREW

'Will I die?' you ask. And so I enter on
The dutiful exposition of that which you
Would rather not know, and I rather not tell you.
To soften my 'Yes' I offer compensations –
Age and fulfilment ('It's so far away;
You will have children and grandchildren by then')
And indifference ('By then you will not care').
No need: you cannot believe me, convinced
That if you always eat plenty of vegetables
And are careful crossing the street you will live for ever.
And so we close the subject, with much unsaid –
This, for instance: Though you and I may die
Tomorrow or next year, and nothing remain
Of our stock, of the unique, preciously-hoarded
Inimitable genes we carry in us,
It is possible that for many generations
There will exist, sprung from whatever seeds,
Children straight-limbed, with clear enquiring voices,
Bright-eyed as you. Or so I like to think:
Sharing in this your childish optimism.

The Eye of the Hurricane (A.H. & A.W. Reed, 1964)

PARTING IS SUCH SWEET SORROW

The room is full of clichés – 'Throw me a crumb'
And 'Now I see the writing on the wall'
And 'Don't take umbrage, dear.' I wish I could.
Instead I stand bedazzled by them all,

Longing for shade. Belshazzar's fiery script
Glows there, between the prints of tropical birds,
In neon lighting, and the air is full
Of crumbs that flash and click about me. Words

Glitter in colours like those gaudy prints:
The speech of a computer, metal-based
But feathered like a cloud of darts. All right.
Your signal-system need not go to waste.

Mint me another batch of tokens: say
'I am in your hands; I throw myself upon
Your mercy, casting caution to the winds.'
Thank you; there is no need to go on.

Thus authorised by your mechanical
Issue, I lift you like a bale of hay,
Open the window wide, and toss you out;
And gales of laughter whirl you far away.

Tigers (Oxford University Press, 1967)

CATTLE IN MIST

A postcard from my father's childhood –
the one nobody photographed or painted;
the one we never had, my sister and I.
Such feeble daughters – couldn't milk a cow
(watched it now and then, but no one taught us).
How could we hold our heads up, having never
pressed them into the warm flank of a beast
and lured the milk down? Hiss, hiss, in a bucket:
routine, that's all. Not ours. That one missed us.

His later childhood, I should say;
not his second childhood – that he evaded
by dying – and his first was Manchester.
But out there in the bush, from the age of ten,
in charge of milking, rounding up the herd,
combing the misty fringes of the forest
(as he would have had to learn not to call it)
at dawn, and again after school, for stragglers;
cursing them; bailing them up; it was no childhood.

A talent-spotting teacher saved him.
The small neat smiling boy (I'm guessing)
evolved into a small neat professor.
He could have spent his life wreathed in cow-breath,
a slave to endlessly refilling udders,
companion of heifers, midwife at their calvings,
judicious pronouncer on milk-yields and mastitis,
survivor of the bull he bipped on the nose
('Tell us again, Daddy!') as it charged him.

All his cattle: I drive them back
into the mist, into the dawn haze
where they can look romantic; where they must
have wandered now for sixty or seventy years.

Off they go, then, tripping over the tree-roots,
pulling up short to lip at a tasty twig,
bumping into each other, stumbling off again
into the bush. He never much liked them.
He'll never need to rustle them back again.

Looking Back (Oxford University Press, 1997)

The yellow crocuses
break open the ochre clay.
It's good to notice them,

you say. We sit together
on the green garden bench
beneath an oak. Quercus

robur. That reassuring
lyricism of the Latin names
displayed on little plaques . . .

I look across the pond.
Carp nuzzle their shadows
on the weeded rocks.

And leaning back, arms
stretched out and then back,
you open up, the body

and its light unsheathed.
The light given up to light,
petals on the water.

Death is similar to this:
your hands are flowering
in that space behind

your head, and listening.
It is almost as though
something else is breathing

quite close by, invisibly.
The mystery of the names . . .
Albizzia. Gleditsia.

Aucuba japonica. And
I am listening, seeing. Seeing,
like someone twice alive.

Stone Moon Dark Water (Sudden Valley Press, 1999)

IM ABENDROT

from THE FOUR LAST SONGS OF RICHARD STRAUSS
AT TAKAHE CREEK ABOVE THE KAIPARA

The far Brynderwyns heave across the harbour,
rising upon the second tide, mountains
in mangrove moving, weaving
the last complexities of the sun. These
are a tangle of reflections. Over them,
the next peninsula shines yellow,
pastoral century of slow change,
and the roofs of pioneers, like beacons, prophesy
the imminence of fishermen, their lights
alive and casting, quick
to be out before the strong tide sucks and runs.

      I sing of our long voyaging,
      and you who led me, at my side;
      I sing the saddest of all things;
      I sing the unaccomplished bride.

The hills will cease to float soon, and the mangroves
ripple themselves away.
The wandering flames of grass will calm, and the cattle
boom night's gullies up and down. My lights
will anchor a headland. Boats will take bearings,
seeking the channel; and then,
the Kaipara will move out.
A shag clap-claps in shallows.
I point the way to an open sea,
though all my doors are closed,
and I within.

      Go slowly, sun. A gentle death

of day is in the birds that wheel
in clouds to their accustomed rest,
and in the racing of the keel

before the racing of the tide,
and in the crowding of dark trees.
I sing the unaccomplished bride.
I sing my death in all of these.

Riding the Pendulum (Oxford University Press, 1973)

THE TALL WIND

He said to them, Look at this: you see
where the tall wind leans against your window-pane?
And they said Yes; the cold has come again.
Which being true, he dared not disagree.

Instead he said, If that wind once more blows
like that, your house will fly away like straw.
But they, of course, had thought of that before.
And also, though he did not dare suppose

they might have done, they'd seen a dead man lain
for laundering on half a fallen tree.
He thought, How strangely that man looks like me;
and said aloud, With luck there'll be no rain . . .

and just as he spoke, it started in to pour.
One of them laughed, and one said, Thar she blows:
we'll find out now what this young charlie knows.
There's a tall wind out there, leaning on our door.

Riding the Pendulum (Oxford University Press, 1973)

New Zealand

So the last day's come at last, the close of my fifteen year –
The end of the hope, an' the struggles, an' messes I've put in
here.
All of the shearings over, the final mustering done, –
Eleven hundred an' fifty for the incoming man, near on.
Over five thousand I drove 'em, mob by mob, down the coast;
Eleven-fifty in fifteen year . . . it isn't much of a boast.

Oh, it's a bad old place! Blown out o' your bed half the nights,
And in summer the grass burnt shiny an' bare as your hand, on
the heights:
The creek dried up by November, and in May a thundering roar
That carries down toll o' your stock to salt 'em whole on the
shore.
Clear'd I have, and I've clear'd an' clear'd, yet everywhere, slap
in your face,
Briar, tauhinu, an' ruin! – God! it's a brute of a place.
. . . An' the house got burnt which I built, myself, with all that
worry and pride;
Where the Missus was always homesick, and where she took
fever, and died.

Yes, well! I'm leaving the place. Apples look red on that
bough.
I set the slips with my own hand. Well – they're the other man's
now.
The breezy bluff: an' the clover that smells so over the land,
Drowning the reek o' the rubbish, that plucks the profit out o'
your hand:
That bit o' Bush paddock I fall'd myself, an' watch'd, each year,
come clean
(Don't it look fresh in the tawny? A scrap of Old-Country
green):
This air, all healthy with sun an' salt, an' bright with purity:

An' the glossy karakas there, twinkling to the big blue twinkling
   sea:
Ay, the broad blue sea beyond, an' the gem-clear cove below,
Where the boat I'll never handle again, sits rocking to and fro:
There's the last look to it all! an' now for the last upon
This room, where Hetty was born, an' my Mary died, an'
   John . . .
Well! I'm leaving the poor old place, and it cuts as keen as a
   knife;
The place that's broken my heart – the place where I've lived
   my life.

Reuben and Other Poems (Constable, 1903)

Alone we are born
  And die alone;
Yet see the red-gold cirrus
  Over snow-mountain shine.

Upon the upland road
  Ride easy, stranger:
Surrender to the sky
  Your heart of anger.

Collected Poems (Oxford University Press, 1979)

BALLAD OF CALVARY STREET

On Calvary Street are trellises
Where bright as blood the roses bloom,
And gnomes like pagan fetishes
Hang their hats on an empty tomb
Where two old souls go slowly mad,
National Mum and Labour Dad.

Each Saturday when full of smiles
The children come to pay their due,
Mum takes down the family files
And cover to cover she thumbs them through,
Poor Len before he went away
And Mabel on her wedding day.

The meal-brown scones display her knack,
Her polished oven spits with rage,
While in Grunt Grotto at the back
Dad sits and reads the Sporting Page,
Then ambles out in boots of lead
To weed around the parsnip bed.

A giant parsnip sparks his eye,
Majestic as the Tree of Life;
He washes it and rubs it dry
And takes it in to his old wife –
'Look Laura, would that be a fit?
The bastard has a flange on it!'

When both were young she would have laughed,
A goddess in her tartan skirt,
But wisdom, age and mothercraft
Have rubbed it home that men like dirt:
Five children and a fallen womb,
A golden crown beyond the tomb.

Nearer the bone, sin is sin,
And women bear the cross of woe,
And that affair with Mrs Flynn
(it happened thirty years ago)
Though never mentioned, means that he
Will get no sugar in his tea.

The afternoon goes by, goes by,
The angels harp above a cloud;
A son-in-law with spotted tie
And daughter Alice fat and loud
Discuss the virtues of insurance
And stuff their tripes with trained endurance.

Flood-waters hurl upon the dyke
And Dad himself can go to town,
For little Charlie on his trike
Has ploughed another iris down.
His parents rise to chain the beast,
Brush off the last crumbs of their lovefeast.

And so these two old fools are left,
A rosy pair in evening light,
To question Heaven's dubious gift,
To hag and grumble, growl and fight:
The love they kill won't let them rest,
Two birds that peck in one fouled nest.

Why hammer nails? Why give no change?
Habit, habit clogs them dumb.
The Sacred Heart above the range
Will bleed and burn till Kingdom Come,
But Yin and Yang won't ever meet
In Calvary Street, in Calvary Street.

Collected Poems (Oxford University Press, 1979)

TOMCAT

This tomcat cuts across the
zones of the respectable
through fences, walls, following
other routes, his own. I see
the sad whiskered skull-mouth fall
wide, complainingly, asking

to be picked up and fed, when
I thump up the steps through bush
at 4 p.m. He has no
dignity, thank God! has grown
older, scruffier, the ash-
black coat sporting one or two

flowers like round stars, badges
of bouts and fights. The snake head
is seamed on top with rough scars:
old Samurai! He lodges
in cellars, and the tight furred
scrotum drives him into wars

as if mad, yet tumbling on
the rug looks female, Turkish-
trousered. His bagpipe shriek at
sluggish dawn dragged me out in
pyjamas to comb the bush
(he being under the vet

for septic bites): the old fool
stood, body hard as a board,
heart thudding, hair on end, at
the house corner, terrible,
yelling at something. They said,
'Get him doctored.' I think not.

Collected Poems (Oxford University Press, 1979)

1

The small grey cloudy louse that nests in my beard
Is not, as some have called it, 'a pearl of God' –

No, it is a fiery tormentor
Waking me at two a.m.

Or thereabouts, when the lights are still on
In the houses in the pa, to go across thick grass

Wet with rain, feet cold, to kneel
For an hour or two in front of the red flickering

Tabernacle light – what He sees inside
My meandering mind I can only guess –

A madman, a nobody, a raconteur
Whom He can joke with – 'Lord,' I ask Him,

'Do You or don't You expect me to put up with lice?'
His silent laugh still shakes the hills at dawn.

Collected Poems (Oxford University Press, 1979)

> Happy the cicadas, for they have silent wives.
>
> XENARCHUS

We call it song. No doubt a handy textbook
would tell me just how it is made:
this thrilling trilling boringly ecstatic
high monotone.

A friction of the scaly parts? Certainly at times
there is a flap of the wings, a spasmodic
brief convulsion; then back to the dentist's drill,
for cicadas the pure lyric joy.

What you sing is love, no question of that:
whether love of the nearest female parked
immobile and dumb, drunk with the heady fume
of manuka bark, of clay;

Or (rather more likely, I think) of life-and-death
together, the consummation, the liebestod:
love of a summer too short to last, of the aching
cold to come.

You make us hear it, you make us feel it too.
Male and female, we are as lightly parked
on our earth bank, we mate and die, we expect to
live longer: but you do not cease to sing.

Occasional Verses (Wai-te-ata Press, 1971)

O Michael, you are at once the enemy
And the chief ornament of our garden,
Scrambling up rose-posts, nibbling at nepeta,
Making your lair where tender plants should flourish,
Or proudly couchant on a sun-warmed stone.

What do you do all night there,
When we seek our soft beds,
And you go off, old roisterer,
Away into the dark?

I think you play at leopards and panthers;
I think you wander on to foreign properties;
But on winter mornings you are a lost orphan
Pitifully wailing underneath our windows;
And in summer, by the open doorway,
You come in pad, pad, lazily to breakfast,
Plumy tail waving, with a fine swagger,
Like a drum-major, or a parish beadle,
Or a rich rajah, or the Grand Mogul.

Collected Poems (Victoria University Press, 1997)

FALL

Autumn, I think, now.

Rose hues assume a deeper intensity.
Little birds flying in from far in the wild bush
Pursue insects boldly even into our parlours.

The play of the winds is less turbulent:
They scatter gently forspent petallage,
And a scent of ripe seeds is borne on their soft gusts.

Today I do not perceive the outcry of young folk;
Perhaps they are helping to get in some harvest,
Or far afield for important ball-games.

Only old men pause by the sunny roadside
Noticing the same sights that I have noticed,
And listening to the same quietness.

We do not regret that we are of ripe years
We do not complain of grey hairs and infirmities
We are drowsy and very ready to fall into deep sleep.

Collected Poems (Victoria University Press, 1997)

The green has come back, the spring green, the new green,
Darling, the young green upon the field willows,
And the gorse on the wild hills was never so yellow,
Together, together, past years we have looked on the scene.

The loved little bird is singing his small song,
Dearest, and whether the trill of the riro
Reminded, we wondered, of joy or of sorrow –
Now I am taught it is tears, it is tears that to spring time belong.

You were laughter, my liking, and frolic, my lost one,
    I must dissemble and smile still for your sake,
    Now that I know how spring time is heart-break,
Now you have left me to look upon all that is lovely, alone.

Collected Poems (Victoria University Press, 1997)

B

TONY BEYER (1948–)

I go with him on the other end
of the chain about the villages

and the money flung with contempt
in the battered hat feeds us both

our act has not changed for years
but lately I find his timing unsure

he snuffles and wags his head while
we work and seems to be listening

to some sly undernote the music
has fashioned for his ears alone

when he grows too weak to travel
one swipe of my big furred arm

will rive him open for a last
unsavoury meal before I am free

Dancing Bear (Melaleuca Press, 1981)

after he was wounded at el mreir
a woman whose sister was married
to the brother of the woman
he would eventually marry
nursed him in the military hospital in alexandria

in her version
he was among eight men so hurt they were
left outside on the porch for the night to decide
and only he lived until morning

he spoke sometimes later
about the injuries of the others
their ranks and branches of service
and what parts of the desert or sky or sea
had been the ruin of them
but never about the sounds he must have heard

The Male Voice (Dead Poets Books, 1998)

COUNTRIES LODGE IN THE BODY

A letter to Maura

This morning I woke
fists clenched, body worn.
All night sleep evaded me.

Shifting my bed from room to room,
head facing west,
then east, stalking sleep.

I woke thinking of land –
how countries lodge in the body
long after you have moved elsewhere.

Salt wind through a beech forest,
sea sounding on a black sand shore,
the sternum a long stretch of earth.

Here, winter bodies
marzipan pale.
Smell of wet manuka, old oilskins.

When we parted,
the new whey scent of fresh sweat,
sky soaking up evening.

This morning I walked
through magnolias
weighted with blossoms,

huge and dove-like,
petals poised
to open and fall away.

bell tongue (Victoria University Press, 1999)

WELLINGTON

A city of cenotaphs and tram-car sonnets . . .
Broad-breasted town, thy swarded mounds
More numerous than Rome's . . . We hang
Our houses out like washing to a breeze
That warns us of Scott's death-wish in the south.

The last colonial outpost . . . Perhaps
The liveliest capital since the Vatican.
Arriving, anchored where Victoria's brigs
Banged bibles and brass cannon. I'd
Marvelled at hotels like pink casinos.

Wharves like sea-side cafes, terraced hills
Of rainbow-bright facades and cubist houses.
The gentleman's convenience in mid-town
I'd taken for a temple, and the people
Splashing in Oriental Bay seemed crowds

Of sun-gods spilt from a Picasso painting.
Let's blame it on the light! I stand
Committed to imaginary landfalls . . .
The back door of a British council house
Could only lead out to the new Jerusalem:
Blake's burning bow was bound to scorch my hand.

My Side of the Story (Mate Books, 1964)

MR MAUI AT BUCKINGHAM PALACE

Dumping the suit of armour my grandfather
was given by Queen Victoria. The fool
even wore it in bed. At the Governor's ball
he looked like Don Quixote. Now
I've chucked it back, over the palace wall.
True, the little Gurkha guard got shirty
but I gave him my black-power stare. You'll
notice I'm wearing my 'Pommie Bastard' T-shirt
and thumping stray bobbies with the jaw-bone club
I tore from an old whore's mouth. Lately
I've developed a sense of history . . .
this visit purges my colonial past.
Soon I'll be looking for a girl to crawl into.
Someone my type . . . a goddess perhaps.
I don't like debs. They're always crossing cool legs.
I like my women wide open. I can't speak fairer than that.

Mr Maui (London Magazine Editions, 1976)

INSTRUCTIONS FOR HOW TO GET AHEAD OF
YOURSELF WHILE THE LIGHT STILL SHINES

If you have a bike, get on it at night
and go to the top of the Brooklyn Hill.

When you reach the top
start smiling – this is Happy Valley Road.

Pedal at first, then let the road take you down
into the dark as black as underground
broken by circles of yellow lowered by the street lights.

As you come to each light
you will notice a figure
racing up behind.
Don't be scared
this is you creeping up on yourself.
As you pass under the light
you will sail past yourself into the night.

Moving House (Victoria University Press, 1989)

THE VISIT

You approach the world
with open arms and hope
it wants you. Hope to be
asked in to sit amongst the
fine furniture. The world is
busy and polite and believes
in independence. You want
to make friends, be
boisterous. You'd expected
something a little more
gregarious but you'll
take a photo anyway to show
your friends. Here it is.
Here's the world on a good
day, turned slightly
away, but this is no
offence, merely the sun was
in its eyes and it turned
briefly to avoid being
blinded by it.

Waiting Shelter (Victoria University Press, 1991)

3

Far on the mountains of pain there may yet be a place
For breath, where the insensate wind is still,
A hollow of stones where you can bow your face
And relax the quivering distended will.

There earth's life will speak to you again,
An insect in the grasses, a meagre bird,
That in that outpost faithfully maintain
The pulse of being so slowly, weakly heard.

And they remain. But you go on, and bear
The frail life farther yet, blindly and slow,
Into the pitiless mountains and the glare
Of deathly light, ceasing to know or care
If you are still man; but the frozen rocks know,
And the white wind massing against you as you go.

Collected Poems (Oxford University Press, 1984)

BREAK AND GO

No one has clean hands,
None a pure heart.
We shall be part of one
Another to life's end
Whether we would or not.
But now break, go,
Let silence fall like snow:
Together we offend.

We hurt and cannot help,
Clinging for old time's sake.
Better to break the ring
And break pride's foolish neck
Than grind each other to dust
In sullen loyalty
To an old love that we
Have steered to shipwreck.

Silence will keep faith –
May be; words ring dead,
And nothing we said remains.
God grant I never see
Or hear of you again.
Is it not enough pain
That your blood beats in my blood?
The rest is vanity.

Collected Poems (Oxford University Press, 1984)

WINTER ANEMONES

The ruby and amethyst eyes of anemones
Glow through me, fiercer than stars.
Flambeaux of earth, their dyes
From age-lost generations burn
Black soil, branches and mosses into light
That does not fail, though winter grip the rocks
To adamant. See, they come now
To lamp me through inscrutable dusk
And down the catacombs of death.

Collected Poems (Oxford University Press, 1984)

B

I have a new scarlet coat and
I look like a fire engine
And I don't give a damn
One should grow old gracefully
Someone said – I don't know who
But I've heard it all my life and
So have you well to hell with that
I refuse to grow old any way
But reluctantly and bold as brass
And when arthritis bites in all
My bones and sleep sulks outside
My bedroom window in the dark
I just toss and turn and scratch
And swear the hours away I'm not
Growing older – it's the stupid
Betrayal of bones and flesh
That makes me feel this way but

Look at me now with springs in
My heels and the wind in my hair
Any moment I'll start whistling
And might even dance you a jig
And stop all the traffic along the
Quay wearing my new scarlet coat
And looking like a fire engine.

Up Here on the Hill (Mallinson Rendel, 1989)

WILD DAISIES

If you love me
Bring me flowers
Wild daisies
Clutched in your fist

Like a torch
No orchids or roses
Or carnations
No florist's bow
Just daisies
Steal them
Risk your life for them
Up the sharp hills
In the teeth of the wind
If you love me
Bring me daisies
Wild daisies
That I will cram
In a bright vase
And marvel at

Up Here on the Hill (Mallinson Rendel, 1989)

TREMORS

People will tell
how it went bone quiet,
how time paused pre-pounce
and the cat bristled.

See, they flutter, the sky jam taut,
hangings to and fro,
cats crouch, absorb,
accuse with dark eyes.

They wear their relief
like 'I Survived' sweatshirts,
fast-forwarding constipated smiles,
their unavoidable inclusion.

In the rattled moment
if the earth is neither
here

                           nor

      there
most people are still.

Precious few jump for
doorways, outdoors
catching hopping hail,
a cupful to deep-freeze.

For most, grouped and alone,
it is the tapping after-shock
and half-thankful wondering
who to phone.

Go Round Power Please (Victoria University Press, 1996)

LOOK HERE

It is morning because the sun has risen.
It is morning because the darkness is
packed off to Europe and because the
clock says so and the radio and the
wet clothes sinking down from the
line begin to be responsible again,
try to shake themselves and face up to
drying and it is morning because the
jug quivers and bubbles and switches itself
off and my fingers force the skin off my
orange, and the blue and white teapot
holds fresh tea, and it is morning because
things to be done line up in front of me and
say, look here.

The Hungry Woman (Victoria University Press, 1997)

C

KATE CAMP (1972–)

Man has made a splendid job of everything.

See him build and locomote himself
capture animals, measure the weather.

From the most unpromising beginnings
he produces useful and beautiful things.

In the afternoon he chews the grass or
lies, a beach of ribby dunes to wash on.

Ingeniously he hides his veins of boys
-enberry, morsels of jelly, choc chips.

Yes man has many secrets he draws out
in treacly strands, hid in his factory,

spinning from filaments a dainty dress which once
was marbles, milk bottles, mirror shards.

Think of the hazard this broken glass was
to the community! It will now cease

to be ugly and dangerous but will
have a sheen rivalling that of silk.

The present century teems with wonder.

Unfamiliar Legends of the Stars (Victoria University Press, 1998)

LOOKING AT KAPITI

December, 1959

Sleep, Leviathan, shouldering the Asian
Night sombre with fear, kindled by one star
Smouldering through fog, while the goaded ocean
Recalls the fury of Te Rauparaha.

Massive, remote, familiar, hung with spray,
You seem to guard our coast, sanctuary
To our lost faith, as if against the day
Invisible danger drifts across the sea.

And yet in the growing darkness you lose
Your friendly contours, taking on the shape
Of the destroyer – dread Moby Dick whose
Domain is the mind, uncharted, without hope.

Without hope, I watch the dark envelop
You and like a light on a foundering ship's
Masthead the star go out, while shoreward gallop
The Four Horsemen of the Apocalypse.

Pocket Collected Poems (Hazard Press, 1996)

ALISTAIR TE ARIKI CAMPBELL (1925–)

GATHERING MUSHROOMS

Dried thistles hide his face.
Look closely –
that's your enemy.
Ants carry away his flesh,
but still he grins.
You know him by his thumbs
round and white,
breaking the earth like mushrooms,
coated with fine sand.

A bony finger flicks a bird
into your face,
daisies snap at your heels,
nostrils
flare in the ground
that you believed was solid –
and a dark wind rides
the whinnying tussock up the hillside.

Gather your mushrooms then,
and if you dare
ignore the thin cries of the damned,
issuing through the gills.

Sick of running away
you drop in the soaking grass.
Through tears
you watch a snail climbing a straw
that creaks and bends
under its weight,
and note how tenderly it lifts
upon its shoulder
the fallen weight of the sky.

Pocket Collected Poems (Hazard Press, 1996)

WAITING FOR THE PAKEHA

Here we are assembled on the bank,
a hundred souls – the remnant of our tribe –
decked out in mats and bearing greenery
to welcome to the pa our Pakeha.

And there's our chief, his club held ready
to give the signal for the show to start,
a sudden blink as of the moon through cloud
the only sign of life on his carved face.

Behind him, with bowed head, her pointed breasts
parting her long black hair, stands his daughter –
an offering to the Pakeha . . . Surely
such loveliness will fetch a crate of muskets.

The scouts we sent to meet the Pakeha
grin at us from the opposite bank,
their heads impaled on stakes. Our enemies
grow bolder every day, and they have guns.

But where is he? Where is the Pakeha?
The elders in their fly-blown dog-skin mats
yearn for their smoky whares – the womb
of Mother Night. Dogs whimper and the children

dream fearfully of ovens as they burrow
into the warmth of their mothers' bodies . . .
The enemy guns are growing more insistent:
we shall not wait again for the Pakeha.

Pocket Collected Poems (Hazard Press, 1996)

MEG CAMPBELL (1937–)

It is the shooting season,
and black swans have found
sanctuary at Pukerua Bay
where three small beaches
lie between the rocks.
This morning, the swans
are riding a gentle swell
and, above them, a rainbow
earthing its colours
in the hill-side, makes us
pause and count them again.
And all day, in the city,
this image remains with us –
black swans, and a rainbow.

A Durable Fire (Te Kotare Press, 1982)

MY COUNTRYWOMAN

She is the Kiwi, the Dodo bird
of the South Seas, weak-eyed,
with heavy legs and arse
and beak that doubles as a weapon –
pecking sharpens her mind.
Violent and amiable, both, she is
often seen at shopping centres
flanked by kids and elderly mother.
Sometimes she is seen in the undergrowth
of jumble sales or Church bazaar,
pressing to the front, her money
extended to buy the tastiest cake.
In the bedroom, at night, she sports
tiny wings – the curious remnant
of her long-lost flight.

A Durable Fire (Te Kotare Press, 1982)

PETER CAPE (1926–1979)

I got a new brown sportscoat,
I got a new pair of grey strides,
I got a new Kiwi haircut,
Bit off the top and short back and sides.

As soon as I've tied up the guri,
As soon as I've broomed out the yard,
As soon as I've hosed down my gumboots,
I'll be living it high and living it hard.

I'm going to climb on to the tractor,
I'm going to belt it out of the gate.
There's a hop on down the hall, and
She starts somewhere 'bout half-past eight.

Hey, look at the sheilas cuttin' the supper.
An' look at the kids sliding over the floor,
And look at the great big bunch of jokers,
Hanging round the door.

They got the teacher to belt the piano;
They got Joe from the store on the drums;
Yeah, we're slick as the Orange in Auckland
For whooping things up and making them hum.

I had a schottische with the tart from the butcher's,
Got stuck for a waltz with the constable's wife;
I had a beer from the keg on the cream-truck,
And the cop had one, too, you can bet your life.

Oh, it's great being out with the jokers,
When the jokers are sparking and bright;
Yeah, it's great giving cheek to the sheilas,
Down the hall on Saturday night.

Peter Cape's Kiwi Ballads (Kiwi Pacific Records Intnl. Ltd., 1960)

In the time of his going
we talked often of the creatures.
There was the snake sleeping on a vine
of dense jasmin alongside the veranda
the rabbit under the house
also the huntsman spider, which leapt
surprising distances to capture bush cockroaches,
a vigilant creature seeing what lay before it
and what had been left behind
all at the same time.

These conversations went on for several hours;
they did not seem avoidance –
the dying man took as much part in them
as anybody else; he was comfortable
as far as we could see or make him.

There were other creatures we discussed
but did not see –
the cane toad sleek within its poison
the leech that possibly
might have been of some temporary help.

We could not come to a decision
that there was no help

The bush maybe had answers
it was keeping quiet about and although its quiet
went on for further than we could imagine
there seemed always the chance that its creatures
would tell us something if we listened hard enough
something more than predators tell their prey
the bush sounds being drawn by our location
meeting place of two winds.

In the time of his going however
the days were bland; we never saw
the counterleaning trees marking the true place
could not discover if the meeting
results in any kind of peace that one can be aware of
and be there at the windless instant.

SUMMER FIRES

In summer the gorse along our ridge
would burn like petrol,
like something Australian, cinematic
in the west.

A green baize door
might recall to me a time
when my mother visited a house of white
beneath a white magnolia.

I was to have a brother.
And I was told, no,
he will never grow like you, not
up.

Of fires, then, of moulting trees
hastelessly shedding profusion
through the shades and glares of noons
innumerably blameless

was my brother born. Blameless
the things which sire us.

Aztec Noon (Victoria University Press, 1992)

Wasn't this the site, asked the historian,
Of the original homestead?
Couldn't tell you, said the cowman;
I just live here, he said,
Working for old Miss Wilson
Since the old man's been dead.

Moping under the bluegums
The dog trailed his chain
From the privy as far as the fowlhouse
And back to the privy again,
Feeling the stagnant afternoon
Quicken with the smell of rain.

There sat old Miss Wilson,
With her pictures on the wall,
The baronet uncle, mother's side,
And one she called The Hall;
Taking tea from a silver pot
For fear the house might fall.

People in the *colonies,* she said,
Can't quite understand . . .
Why, from Waiau to the mountains
It was all father's land.

She's all of eighty said the cowman,
Down at the milking-shed.
I'm leaving here next winter.
Too bloody quiet, he said.

The spirit of exile, wrote the historian,
Is strong in the people still.

He reminds me rather, said Miss Wilson,
Of Harriet's youngest, Will.

Early Days Yet, Poems 1941–1997 (Auckland University Press, 1997)

Mock up again, summer, the sooty altars
Between the sweltering tides and the tin gardens,
All the colours of the stained bow windows.
Quick, she'll be dead on time, the single
Actress shuffling red petals to this music,
Percussive light! So many suns she harbours
And keeps them jigging, her puppet suns,
All over the dead hot calm impure
Blood noon tide of the breathless bay.

Are the victims always so beautiful?

Pearls pluck at her, she has tossed her girls
Breast-flowers for keepsakes now she is going
For ever and astray. I see her feet
Slip into the perfect fit the shallows make her
Purposefully, sure as she is the sea
Levels its lucent ruins underfoot
That were sharp dead white shells, that will be sands.
The shallows kiss like knives.

Always for this
They are chosen for their beauty.

Wristiest slaughterman December smooths
The temple bones and parts the grey-blown brows
With humid fingers. It is an ageless wind
That loves with knives, it knows our need, it flows
Justly, simply as water greets the blood,
And woody tumours burst in scarlet spray.
An old man's blood spills bright as a girl's
On beaches where the knees of light crash down.
These dying ejaculate their bloom.

Can anyone choose
And call it beauty? – The victims
Are always beautiful.

Early Days Yet, Poems 1941–1997 (Auckland University Press, 1997)

LONE KAURI ROAD

Too many splashes, too many gashes,
too big and too many holes in the west wall:
one by one the rectangles blazed and blacked where the
sun fell out of its frame, the time of the day
hung round at a loose end, lopsided.

It was getting desperate, even a fool could see,
it was feverish work, impossible to plug them all.
Even a fool, seeing the first mountain fall
out not into the sea or the smoking west but into
the places where these had been, could see the spider
brushed up, dusted, shovelled into the stove, and
how fast his legs moved, without the least surprise.

A tui clucked, shat, whistled thrice.
My gaze was directed where the branch had been.
An engine fell mute into the shadow of the valley
where the shadow had been.

Early Days Yet, Poems 1941–1997 (Auckland University Press, 1997)

MOULES À LA MARINIÈRE

It took the sun six hours to peel
the sea from the gut, black underwater
dries out grey underfoot, 'cleft for me'

to look down. The dull thought of drowning
ebbed with the flood, this orifice entices
wide open, gargling, warm at the lips.

Not all the way down. The deepest
secretions don't drain, still you can 'feel'
what's below the bottom of the tide,

knowing more than's good for you: seabed
rock wetted perpetually with spectral
colours, quotations lifted from

life into a stony text, epigraphies
remembering shot-silk offals, trapped
green weed, petrifying mauves,

muddy cysts, mucus, your own interior
furnishings, glands, genitalia
of the slit reef spilling seawards:

walls of scabby pink, sprayed-on starfish,
gluey limpets, linings of the gut which
swallowing a wave throws up an ocean,

it smells of your nature, sickishly.
Hold on tight, by one hand, stripping
off the mussels, quick! with the other

into the bag, don't count cut bleeding
fingers. The tide scrapes the bottom,
blinded and a bit fouled with sand

the slack of the swell drools, fills, empties,
refills, your jeans are sodden
to the crotch, that's wet enough, the bag's

heavy enough: do you really want more
mussels, old swimmer, do you need
more drowning lessons? Here it comes, one

ten-foot wave after another, it's
all yours now and it's up to you down
in the gut and the blind gut

in the wet of your eye gorging
moules à la marinière,
an enormous weight! Nothing to the

tonnages of water lightly climbing
your back. Picked off alive and
kicking in the rip, did you 'feel'

unaccountably unsurprised by
how natural it all is, in the end,
no problem, the arms and legs have only

to exercise the right allowed by law,
last words, the succinctest body-language.
You're innocent. The sea does the rest.

Early Days Yet, Poems 1941–1997 (Auckland University Press, 1997)

FROST AT NIGHT

Pierce and crackle of stars
Over low roofs, ice-encrusted,
Sparks ablaze
In the sky's chimney;
Amethyst walls,
Roof-iron creaking,
And the washing suspended rigid.

The strokes of the town clock
Spread evenly and far,
Steadily
As rings
Widening
On a lulled
Pond.

Eleven

Twelve

Hoot of a train far off.

Afterwards
The ghost town.
In the forsaken streets
Frost only.
A lunar
Stillness.

Day Book (Caxton Press, 1966)

PHOTOGRAPHS OF PIONEER WOMEN

You can see from their faces
Life was not funny,
The streets, when there were streets,
Tugging at axles,
The settlement ramshackle as a stack of cards.
And where there were no streets, and no houses,
Save their own roof of calico or thatch,
The cows coming morning and afternoon
From the end-of-world swamp,
Udders cemented with mud.

There is nothing to equal pioneering labour
For wrenching a woman out of shape,
Like an old willow, uprooted, thickening.
See their strong arms, their shoulders broadened
By the rhythmical swing of the axe, or humped
Under loads they donkeyed on their backs.
Some of them found time to be photographed,
With bearded husband, and twelve or thirteen children,
Looking shocked, but relentless,
After first starching the frills in their caps.

Walking on the Snow (Caxton Press, 1976)

ICELAND POPPIES

You ask me
    What I am saying
    In my poems.
What am I saying?
    That everything
    Is falling from us,
    We, too, are falling;

And so this day, this
    Hour, with the sun shining
    In its customary fashion
    And the wind blowing the trees,
    You and I,
    Sitting behind windows
    Discussing poems,
This moment, every moment, falls,
    Is falling.

More precious
Than any fiery diamond
Is the flowering human heart,
    Opening like a poppyhead
    And like a poppy falling.

Steps of the Sun (Caxton Press, 1979)

THE GUIDES

JOHN DICKSON (1944–)

from COUNTING THE SEEDS

1

in most of the love poems I've read
the couplings always take place amongst long grass
yet the lovers never notice the grass
how the seed head curves, how it sways in a wind
sometimes, exceptions
the couplings take place amongst lupins
which are always in flower
which throw out a scent which is almost unbearable
yet the lovers never notice
being far too intent on finding their own face in the other
in a few of the poems
the lovers see a mole on a throat or the way a hand releases itself
as though it had been holding some kind of bird
and rightly such visions are celebrated by the poet
in fewer still of the poems
the lovers are thrown forward by powers that lie within
those monsters, their ancestors
who are dead, who are dead, who are dead
but who are there
watching from behind the trees
pathetic voyeurs brimming with jealousy and rage and grief
for the lovers are living and amorous amongst the grass
And in those poems, if we are lucky
not the poet only, but the lovers themselves understand
why their innocent souls are howling in their throats
and by that understanding
come to have no fear of the ancestral darkness
that lightens their bodies
that throws them forward towards each other
the jealousy, the rage, the grief
the ancestors that serve the lovers
that guide their lives until the time they come to rest

What happened on the way to Oamaru (Untold Press, 1986)

for C.B.

That day we walked on the Peninsula
Took care we'd not forget it. The sky was grey,
And grey the sea, and both flat calm in the still
Fresh February air as we climbed each hill
And skirted the beaches, watching the sea unroll
Along the shore its everlasting scroll.
As if good health and weather and such a walk
And friends so close there seemed no need to talk
Were not enough, we saw from the cliff-top
Muttonbirds flying north without a stop
All day, steadily winging above the water
As though they fled from some impending slaughter
In multitudes like nameless refugees
By some magnetic compass of heartsease
Drawn onwards.
                          We had lunch by a little stream
With only our snapping fire to break the dream
Of cloud and tussock and gull. One more delight
Waited until, with Sandymount in sight,
We found a penguin out – it was the stale
Odour of fish and brine that told the tale.
Among the clashing flax of a rocky, wild
Cove he pondered us with questioning, mild
And yellow eyes; then oddly waddled away.
This is my sharpest memory of that day,
Except the mist that made your dark head hoary
Like a ripe seer from some Bible story;

The bellbird clearing his throat in the wet bush
To sing more sweetly than an evening thrush
His silver notes, each one a poet's word,
And the shining cuckoo that we thought we heard.

Windfalls & Other Poems (The Nag's Head Press, 1983)

I grow tired of excess
Billowing like delirium eiderdowns
Like cream buns and true love.
Yes.
I shall give up butter
And love letters
Not to mention French
And the pill.
My conversation will
Grow spare and precise
My legs carry me further out
Along my life
Alert and upright. Private. Possibly deaf.
And I will die
Very neatly and quietly
At dusk, I'd guess
With my papers in order
And my washing folded.
Yes.

EILEEN DUGGAN (1894–1972)

The tides run up the Wairau
That fights against their flow.
My heart and it together
Are running salt and snow.

For though I cannot love you,
Yet, heavy, deep, and far,
Your tide of love comes swinging,
Too swift for me to bar.

Some thought of you must linger,
A salt of pain in me,
For oh what running river
Can stand against the sea?

Selected Poems (Victoria University Press, 1994)

WHEN IN STILL AIR

When in still air the planets shake
Like springs about to flow,
A wind from off Australia
Is gathering to blow.

When the grey-warbler sings close in
Upon the driest noon,
A cloud brewed from the Tasman
Will bring a rainy moon.

And I who have my signs of you
Am weatherwise in vain.
Oh you are gale and wet to me,
But come, my wind and rain.

Selected Poems (Victoria University Press, 1994)

PLAGIARISM

My quest lies far across the hidden waters;
The lands that touch the fairways are all charted,
But better dock than claim another's headland,
Though finds are few now!

I know that it is lying on the sea-rim,
As tender and as dusky as a plumbough;
In cold of words and watches of the spirit,
I comb the oceans.

And if I fail I will have had the thunder,
The bursting, bellying hours of rip and glory,
When the dumb sea lifts up its myriad dew-laps
Of lowing oxen.

But oh the heady joy if I shall find it,
The telling it as if a court were listening,
And I a Spanish sailor with an island,
'Sire, deign to take it!'

Selected Poems (Victoria University Press, 1994)

The worst burn is to come
Though countries blaze like bush,
One moment running song,
The next a blackened hush.

What though the bush-fire's flames
Whirl like a high sunspot,
By paddock suckling seed,
Its roar is soon forgot.

But not so soon by all
For fear is deeper bound.
Though loam may cease to catch,
Peat burns underground.

Selected Poems (Victoria University Press, 1994)

LAURIS EDMOND (1924–2000)

More and more she cries, at two years
old, and more again – more plums more
trees more nests and eggs (and squawking
hens) more pips and melons dribbling
from more lips, more dancing on the roof
more night more day, sun splintering
through cracks of early morning doors,
more floors more bare feet curling on
their woody sheen, more arms and elbows
toes and breasts, more white and smooth
more round and small, more slips of
grassy tips and petal shine, more
gold and black and rosy, smell of feathers
warm, wet, more scrape of gravel, kiss
of dust, more soft sour sharp-sweet,
more shooting stars more midnights,
milk and apples, mountains, cats' meows
and mornings – more, she says. And now.

Wellington Letter (Mallinson Rendel, 1980)

The raspberries they gave us for dessert
were delicious, sharp-tasting and furry,
served in tiny white bowls; you spooned cream
on to mine explaining I'd find it sour.
The waitress with huge eyes and a tuft
of hair pinched like a kewpie so wanted
to please us she dropped two plates as
she swooped through the kitchen door.
No one could reassure her. Snow was falling;
when you spoke, across the narrow white
cloth I could scarcely hear for the distance
nor see you through floating drifts.

Then the tall aunt brought out her dog,
a small prickly sprig like a toy; we put on
our coats and in the doomed silence Chekhov
the old master nodded at us from the wings.
At the last my frozen lips would not
kiss you, I could do nothing but talk
to the terrible little dog: but you
stood still, your polished shoes swelling up
like farm boots. There are always some
who must stay in the country when others
are going to Moscow. Your eyes were
a dark lake bruised by the winter trees.

Catching It (Oxford University Press, 1983)

TEMPO

In the first month I think
it's a drop in a spider web's
necklace of dew

at the second a hazel-nut; after,
a slim Black-eyed Susan demurely folded
asleep on a cloudy day

then a bush-baby silent as sap
in a jacaranda tree, but blinking
with mischief

at five months it's an almost-caught
flounder flapping back
to the glorious water

six, it's a song
with a chorus of basses: seven, five grapefruit
in a mesh bag that bounces on the hip
on a hot morning down at the shops

a water melon next – green oval
of pink flesh and black seeds, ripe
waiting to be split by the knife

nine months it goes faster, it's a bicycle
pedalling for life over paddocks
of sun
no, a money-box filled with silver half-crowns
a sunflower following the clock
with its wide-open grin
a storm in the mountains, spinning rocks
down to the beech trees
three hundred feet below
– old outrageous Queen Bess's best dress
starched ruff and opulent tent of a skirt
packed with ruffles and lace
no no, I've remembered, it's a map
of intricate distinctions

purples for high ground burnt umber
for foothills green for the plains
and the staggering blue
of the ocean beyond
waiting and waiting and
aching
with waiting

no more alternatives! Suddenly now
you can see my small bag of eternity
pattern of power
my ace my adventure
my sweet-smelling atom
my planet, my grain of miraculous dust
my green leaf, my feather
my lily my lark
look at her, angels –
this is my daughter.

Seasons & Creatures (Oxford University Press, 1986)

IN POSITION

I want to tell you about time, how strangely
it behaves when you haven't got much of it left:
after 60 say, or 70, when you'd think it would

find itself squeezed so hard that like melting
ice it would surely begin to shrink, each day
looking smaller and smaller – well, it's not so.

The rules change, a single hour can grow huge
and quiet, full of reflections like an old river,
its slow-turning eddies and whirls showing you

every face of your life in a fluid design –
your children for instance, how you see them
deepened and changed, not merely by age, but by

time itself, its wide and luminous eye; and you
realise at last that your every gift to them – love,
your very life, should they need it – will not

and cannot come back; it wasn't a gift at all
but a borrowing, a baton for them to pass on in
their turn. Look, there they are in this

shimmering distance, rushing through their kind
of time, moving faster than you yet not catching up.
You're alone. And slowly you begin to discern

the queer outline of what's to come: the bend in
the river beyond which, moving steadily, head up
(you hope), you will simply vanish from sight.

A Matter of Timing (Auckland University Press, 1996)

OLD HAT SONG

for Harriet

I was driven up in the back
seat in my old hat –
my new hat then –
red, yellow and black,
the team colours –
wearing my sign on my head,
a sleeve of heart notes
in a record of the past.

I sat on the road in my old hat,
my old hat then,
the walls of cops who hugged
us in, a big, unfriendly
hat to hold unruly citizens,
the contained contained,
buying trouble, as the saying is,
from the counter of
the counter-sign.

'Old Hat' – my daughter's
abbreviated name,
Citizen Hat, with hat
and cane, Citizen Kane,
the one for whom the future is
coming up, up and coming,
comeuppance and getting it,
rosebud by any other name
returned to origin.

Letters & Paragraphs (Caxton Press, 1987)

DAVID EGGLETON (1952–)

Rumours of the death of the author are greatly exaggerated.
There's time to drive round the writer's block once more,
to re-visit sacred inkwells, to download a library of human bookends,
to return to sender flaming letterbombs posted by hotshot critics.

In the earnest vowels of the Shaky Isles plots bloom.
A handkerchief scrap of native bush folds into a hip pocket,
clouds twink out mountains, rain crosshatches hills,
waterspouts rise over the sea like twisting signatures.

Novels groan under the weight of their purple prose,
plays are rarefied body chemistry, poems astronomical physics.
Short stories beach on an agent's desk, fetching up without purpose,
naming a ballpark figure next to an hourglass.

A finishing school of novelists, educated to excellence
by a prescription of award judges pronouncing sentences
with distinction, thumbs the edges of a parallel text.
Enlightenment's the glow-worm glimmer of a far-off town.

Static ghostwriters howl in the transmission frequencies.
Reincarnations of Katherine Mansfield, figments of ambition,
write at will, aiming for the pupils of our eyes.
In the Canterbury dustbowl, dust coalesces into a society of authors.

Empty Orchestra (Auckland University Press, 1995)

TAKAPUNA BEACH

A radiant glut of water, a marbled ocean,
luminous like the glittering green heart
of a pounamu carving revolving in the mind;

Aotearoa's a dreamboat on a perfect ocean,
the America's Cup's found in a cornflakes packet,
a runabout carousels loudly round a ruffled yacht;

daylight's ferris wheel turns, the ocean burns,
silky tendrils of surf, all gurgle and fizz,
dry out into sand and scrunched shell;

a bounty of boutiques smelling of ocean,
a breeze is stroking the back of Takapuna Beach
disappearing into the sun's gift-wrap of glare;

flung up above the rim of the ocean into silence,
the evening moon glows orange like barbecue carbonettes,
the sea goes on writing summer's outline in foam.

Empty Orchestra (Auckland University Press, 1995)

AFTERNOON TEA

They have bought a pony for the child; I have not seen it,
Except clearer than dawn upon my inner eye:
They have bought a small dull pony, and discuss it
At the table while the worrying sun goes down.
But then there is the affair at the last hunt, the scene,
The old man swearing before the cars and the ladies;
And the great fence where Mrs Thompson fell.

But the tea itself; I had forgotten it:
In my first rush I had forgotten the flower,
The aesthetic culmination of a civilized mind;
I had forgotten the cream cakes and the culinary art
The silver teapot and the tasteful wear,
The throbbing lifeblood of our conversation.

The sun collapses, and the leaves fall
As if there were no reason for their falling;
The sun faints in seclusion, and the old pines
Try their hardest to withhold her last jazzy rays
Lest those sipping tea should think her insane
And dissect her as minutely as the neighbour's ways.
The opossum coughs politely; some Satanic spider
Nibbles delicately at his frozen insect;
The cow lifts its tail, and the old dog
Retires behind her kennel lest the others see her.

While the silver steams and the cups clack
While the pony stands in silent tribulation:
While the world spins into darkness and winter descends
There is afternoon tea in the drawing room
And the cackle of empty cups in an obsequious silence.

Landfall 31 (September 1954)

FINDING THE ANCESTORS

for Brigit Pike

Mangonui, Northland

It starts with paspalum and a grave
stone tucked away in high grass.
The wood has weathered and grows
colour in spreading lichen. The date
is an indentation three fingers wide.
The name's been wept out. It was hard
country and only the shape is there
rounded as hills or the church window
blank in all that blue glare of sky
just down the hill round the corner
in the lee of the tree that holds its own
stories. Only the freezias give something
away. A woman perhaps writing a tale
in the planting of bulbs. The tree nods
the wind whistles a tune you think
you've heard before, but across the bay
it's whipped all trace of landfall
away. There are few details.

Talking Pictures – Selected Poems (HeadworX, 2000)

MARGARET ESCOTT (1908-1977)

I have never much *cared* for wattle blossom
Old Mrs Witherspoon said
The Maoris, you know, will not bring it inside
Or was that something I read?
In any case it has a thickish scrambled-egg appearance
Messy to wash from the breakfast plate
And when it dies the little balls are quite hard, quite cruel,
Perhaps I exaggerate.
But I am not as simple as I sound and there were occasions
When poor Arthur was alive –
Arthur was my late husband – when he was in bed
Next door with my niece, he died
You know, leaving us all in *such* an embarrassing position
In so many ways
His, mine, the family way, we are a close family
I sometimes think *too* close,
Families with a deep understanding are so vulnerable
It is family pride I suppose
Nevertheless I have to admit there were a number of occasions
When I was making my tea
That I felt considerable gratitude for the wattle blossom
The fluff of it plumping the tree
Outside the kitchen window on winter mornings
So that I was unable to see
Into the bedroom window next door, it faced this way, I was born
Clear-sighted unfortunately
Also I was reckoned a good shot, what an odd way of putting it
But I *was* a Good Shot
(Poor Arthur used to say so in our earlier days, generous of him
Because he was Not)
And in summer the wattle tree branches bare of blossom
Opened to provide
An irresistible target a possible impossible to miss
A matter of family pride
Again! One would prefer not to speak of it

But alas one grows old and speaks in spite of one's self
Not really knowing
What it is about wattle blossom one likes or dislikes
Dear, must you be going?
I think perhaps you should these Spring evenings are deceptive
And though here one lies
Helpless, old women are deceptive too. Take the wattle blossom
with you, dear,
Before it dies.

*Separation and/or Greetin*g (Auckland University Press, 1980)

Wandering above a sea of glass
    in the soft April weather,
wandering through the yellow grass
    where the sheep stand and blether;
roaming the cliffs in the morning light,
    hearing the gulls that cry there,
not knowing where I'll sleep tonight,
    not much caring either.

I haven't got a stiver
    the tractor's pinched my job,
I owe the bar a fiver
    and the barman fifteen bob;
the good times are over,
    the monkey-man has foreclosed,
the woman has gone with the drover,
    not being what I supposed.

I used to get things spinning,
    I used to dress like a lord,
mostly I came out winning,
    but all that's gone by the board;
my pants have lost their creases,
    I've fallen down on my luck,
the world has dropped to pieces
    everything's come unstuck.

Roaming the cliffs in the morning light,
    hearing the gulls that cry there,
not knowing where I'll sleep tonight,
    not much caring either,
wandering above a sea of glass
    in the soft April weather,
wandering through the yellow grass
    close to the end of my tether.

Selected Poems (Victoria University Press, 1995)

SONG AT SUMMER'S END

Down in the park the children play
rag-happy through the summer day
with dirty feet and freckled faces,
laughing, fighting, running races.
Dull against the smoky skies
the summer's heavy burden lies,
leaden leaves on tired trees
lacking supple limbs like these.

The skyline shows the shape of life,
tomorrow's world of sweat and strife,
fifty stacks and one grey steeple.
Down the street come factory people,
folk who used to play on swings,
dodging chores and apron-strings
to wrestle on the grass and run
barefoot with the fleeting sun.

Some of the kids are sailing boats;
the first leaf drops unheeded, floats
and dances on the muddy pond.
Shadows from the world beyond
lengthen, sprawl across the park;
day rolls onward towards the dark.
From the clock-tower, wreathed in smoke,
Time speaks gravely, stroke on stroke.

Selected Poems (Victoria University Press, 1995)

A FAREWELL

What is there left to be said?
There is nothing we can say,
nothing at all to be done
to undo the time of day;
no words to make the sun
roll east, or raise the dead.

I loved you as I love life:
the hand I stretched out to you
returning like Noah's dove
brought a new earth to view,
till I was quick with love;
but Time sharpens his knife,

Time smiles and whets his knife,
and something has got to come out
quickly, and be buried deep,
not spoken or thought about
or remembered even in sleep.
You must live, get on with your life.

Selected Poems (Victoria University Press, 1995)

UNFINISHED CROSSWORD

If they say:
you may find a friend
in the least likely of places,
I have, here –
fifteen across, ataahua, the beautiful one;
and here – six across – aperira,
the month of the leaf fall;

here – eleven down – aue!
and all the gods crying
in all the places
that ever were & still
                    & still do;

and here – five down – atua,
the gods calling your god,
like the candle flame
and the star in the wide night –
a beckoning.

Unfinished Crossword (Hazard Press, 1990)

ALUN FALCONER

The lizard lies tongue poised
On the twig's dull gold;
Settling, the butterfly's
Brown velvet wings fold.

The white noon sun burns dim;
No jungle birds sound;
Leaves heavy fall with heat
Down to the swamp ground.

Men wan and damp with sweat
In the green vines tense:
Life is utterly dead,
But the guns commence.

War Poems and Lyrics (Harry H. Tombs Ltd, 1946)

CREED

I believe in
the gingerbread man.
Who wouldn't run,
given the circumstances?

But not the Father,
not the Son.

I believe in
forgiveness.

But not in sin.

I believe in
communion:
bread wine
apples and us all
happy at table.

But not in saints.

I believe in
life. You have to,
don't you, being alive?

But not everlasting.

Those immortelles, petals
fallen like yellow teeth
in the tomb, bearing the
form of flowers.

But not the scent,
not the breath.

The Inhabited Initial (Auckland University Press, 1999)

WHAT IT'S LIKE

Well, it's kind of like
you're hanging over a
steep drop, fingers
cracking on some old
root or other and below
there's sand or river,
boulders worn to solid
spheres, and you say to
yourself, 'Now, I could
let go.' And what do
you know?

You do.

And then, it's kind of like
singing with your feet off
the pedals, bush lining a
damp black road downhill
to the corner and a creek
like a crowd hanging about
in dappled shade for you
to whistle by.

And then, it's kind of like
lying on a hillside, sun
full on and a gum tree
rattling away like streamers,
and there's a whole kind of
shining party going on,
and you're at it.

The Inhabited Initial (Auckland University Press, 1999)

LOSING THE WORDS

There are
rumours
of words that were,
words that
have gone
from dictionaries.
The names
of strange
slow birds
no one living has
seen
are gone.
The word
for *water to*
catch in
the hand and drink
and
that for *rich*
earth nourishing
families
no one
remembers.
Forest is slipping
away.

I think
of the word
green
and I am afraid.

A Talent for Flight (Steele Roberts, 1999)

THE KEA SPEAKS FROM THE DUNEDIN BOTANICAL GARDENS

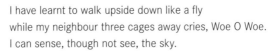

JANET FRAME (1924–)

I have learnt to walk upside down like a fly
while my neighbour three cages away cries, Woe O Woe.
I can sense, though not see, the sky.

I too, like you, have a ceiling of wire to my aspirations,
while the peach-faced lovebirds huddle together close to
    the earth
and the wekas move like small brown brooms through
    the rushes.

If you were to write a poem about me you would say, Pity
the kea's imprisonment. But it would be yourself you
    pitied
in your own prison, for though you can both sense and
    see the sky
you have not yet learned to walk upside down like a fly.

The Pocket Mirror (Pegasus Press, 1967)

RAIN ON THE ROOF

My nephew sleeping in a basement room
has put a sheet of iron outside his window
to recapture the sound of rain falling on the roof.

I do not say to him, The heart has its own comfort for grief.
A sheet of iron repairs roofs only. As yet unhurt by the demand
that change and difference never show, he is still able
to mend damages by creating the loved rain-sound
he thinks he knew in early childhood.

Nor do I say, In the travelling life of loss
iron is a burden, that one day he must find
within himself in total darkness and silence
the iron that will hold not only the lost sound of the rain
but the sun, the voices of the dead, and all else that has gone.

The Pocket Mirror (Pegasus Press, 1967)

ANNE FRENCH (1956–)

CRICKET

All weekend it rained. Heavy spring
rain; the cricket went badly; I spent
most of the weekend up a ladder trying
to paint, trying to get
our boys to score on a dull pitch.
The phone rang, once or twice.

That was how it appeared. The difference
between wanting something, and not
is imperceptible. You can't look
at it with fibre optics, measure it in ohms.
No one could tell, for instance, I burned
waiting for a particular call for which

nothing else would do. Lust
is mostly of the highly differentiated sort.
A particular memory at the base of the spine
here a fullness, here fingers,
add up to a bit on the side – not enough,
just ones and twos on a pitch with no lift.

All Cretans are Liars (Auckland University Press, 1987)

The way to begin is to believe
that you are dead. So I believe it.
The house stinks of compassion. Spring

flowers I picked from the garden
yesterday bleed their humourless
obvious fragrance into the cold air.

I snicked off their unresisting heads,
arranged them without a flicker of pity.
I had to hammer the tough daphne stems

to make them drink. Now, though it's not
yet morning, I lie awake practising
the new words I have learned,

checking my vocabulary for its prudent
omissions. You are dead, and the words
for whole categories of experience

are obsolete. 'Loss,' I begin, 'so this
is loss,' letting the words splash all over me
like the blind and deaf child learning language.

Cabin Fever (Auckland University Press, 1990)

THE MAGPIES

When Tom and Elizabeth took the farm
The bracken made their bed,
And *Quardle oodle ardle wardle doodle*
The magpies said.

Tom's hand was strong to the plough
Elizabeth's lips were red,
And *Quardle oodle ardle wardle doodle*
The magpies said.

Year in year out they worked
While the pines grew overhead,
And *Quardle oodle ardle wardle doodle*
The magpies said.

But all the beautiful crops soon went
To the mortgage-man instead,
And *Quardle oodle ardle wardle doodle*
The magpies said.

Elizabeth is dead now (it's years ago);
Old Tom went light in the head;
And *Quardle oodle ardle wardle doodle*
The magpies said.

The farm's still there. Mortgage corporations
Couldn't give it away.
And *Quardle oodle ardle wardle doodle*
The magpies say.

Enter Without Knocking (Pegasus Press, 1971)

THISTLEDOWN

from SINGS HARRY

Once I followed horses
And once I followed whores
And marched once with a banner
For some great cause,
          Sings Harry.
But that was thistledown planted on
     the wind.

And once I met a woman
All in her heart's spring,
But I was a headstrong fool
Heedless of everything
          Sings Harry.
– I was thistledown planted on the
     wind.

Mustering is the life:
Freed of fears and hopes
I watch the sheep like a pestilence
Pouring over the slopes,
          Sings Harry.
And the past is thistledown planted
     on the wind.

Dream and doubt and the deed
Dissolve like a cloud
On the hills of time.
Be a man never so proud,
          Sings Harry.
He is only thistledown planted on
     the wind.

Enter Without Knocking (Pegasus Press, 1971)

THE END

from ARAWATA BILL

It got you at last, Bill,
The razor-edge that cut you down
Not in the gullies, nor on the pass
But in a bed in town.

RIP where no gold lies
But in your own questing soul
Rich in faith and a wild surmise.

You should have been told
Only in you was the gold:
Mountains and rivers paid you no fee,
Mountain melting to the river,
River to the sea.

Enter Without Knocking (Pegasus Press, 1971)

SOLITARY DRINKER

Standing in the same old place
He thought 'I know that silly face.'
And there beneath the spirits shelf
The mirror showed his silly self.

He saw himself with some surprise
A sorry sod with headlamp eyes.
AFORE YE GO the slogan read,
But he stayed on and stared ahead.

'I cannot stand this blasted place,
I cannot stand my blasted face.'

The public bar was through the hall:
It had no mirrors on the wall.

Enter Without Knocking (Pegasus Press, 1971)

G

KATHLEEN GRATTAN

The builder said,

> 'I'd paint it white.
> Front doors are special.
> Dark brown forbids
> but white suggests
> a shaft of light,
> says Welcome Stranger.'

> (He was a bit of a philosopher,
> had a ready wit.)

A friend who favoured terracotta said,

> 'Be bold – it glows like red
> has a subtler warmth
> but still suggests
> the campfire welcome.'

'Kauri,' said the brown man,

> 'polished and panelled
> knockered with brass.
> Tane the great one
> drawn by its glow
> will turn the handle
> with familiar fingers,
> linger in the shadows.'

> Unconvinced
> (old gods disturb me)
> I held a summit meeting
> with my heart.
> 'I'd beat more easily
> in green   pine green,'
> said heart.
> 'Right,' I answered,
> 'you're the boss.
> Let's start.'

The Music of What Happens (Writers and Artists Press, Auckland, 1987)

THE SNAG

Your eyes resembled wells, gazelles,
    Or stars, as rhyme dictates.
I'll grant you all hyperboles
    From Chaucer down to Yeats.

Your tresses, like a waterfall
    Or woven sunlight, shimmer;
Your body's on the Milo Plan –
    Perhaps, I fancy, slimmer.

Yet 'twas not unrequited love,
    Or search for simile,
Or building hopeless fancies, gave
    Insomnia to me.

Rather, this paradox remains
    To sabotage my sleep;
What made you lovely as a flower
    And silly as a sheep?

A Selection of Poems, Songs and Short Stories (The Gisborne
Herald, 1985)

TRIOLET

I wrote my love a triolet
That burned, as many do,
With ardour, but I now regret
I wrote my love a triolet.

Today a lighted match I set
To all our billet-doux:

I wrote my love a triolet
That burned, as many do.

A Selection of Poems, Songs and Short Stories (The Gisborne
Herald, 1985)

A VISION AT WARRINGTON BEACH

for Sandra

We are such old
friends, one hundred
years equal between us,

standing on the edge
of the sea rocking weed.

My narrow feet
are barred brown by sun
through my sandals,

the left foot slightly
longer than the right,

the right ear slightly
lower than the left

and a tiny barb
from a dentist's probe
broken off in my jaw.

I tell you these things
so you will recognise
the body.

You say you have passed
through the bleeding,
it has all stopped
for you and for a year

and we throw up our arms
and cheer and I say, well,
I might just start
a baby, *jesus!*

and we crack up
and fall about laughing
in the sucking swell,

BERNADETTE HALL (1945–)

more than half in love,
the both of us,

with that big fat woman
flapping her arms
in a floral tent dress,

and especially
her strong thick ankles.

Still Talking (Victoria University Press, 1997)

POEM IN THE MATUKITUKI VALLEY

I know some things
like you'd rather have seen a rotary
clothesline in my garden than roses

and when I dedicated my book of poems
to you, you hammed it up, mock horror,
with 'Jesus, what next!'

So coming down from the mountains,
when Rae asked me what you would have thought
of it all, the grandeur, the excess,

the jade water, the yellow starred flats,
the black peaks with snow like orca leaping,
I had to say that I didn't have a clue,

perhaps something like *what a fuss about nothing!*

and now at night, as the comet works its way
across the greybright sky, I see no sign
that you like Caesar have become a god,

you are far too reliable to be a god,

but rather the gauzy face of a woman,
hair streaming, running with a baby in her arms,
saving me again and again from the burning house.

Still Talking (Victoria University Press, 1997)

MICHAEL HARLOW (1937–)

from POEM THEN, FOR LOVE

2

The way light swarms over
your shoulders.
The day is remarkable that lifts
the town to walk on stilts.
The sun wheels down,
windows shine.

In the crowns of flowers
small fires leap; seeds spill
in the bright air.
Like planets spinning
into sight, passatempo our bodies
turn the hours.

For love your hair sings,
and earth's curve.
For love I pour light
into your body like this –
oh, there is music to be heard,
and just now.

Vlaminck's Tie (Auckland University Press/Oxford University Press,
1985)

CASSANDRA'S DAUGHTER

Cassy for short.
We're discussing the colour green
and why. And how last night
in her dreamtime a wooden-horse
appeared. And look – how the wind
puts shivers in the water;
shaking the keys in their locks.
Only five years old, she is
already in love with how
one word wants another
with astonishing ease.
Inside the alphabet now,
inside the lining of a word
she asks me as we sit
on the garden wall under
a plum-coloured sun: why were you
born at seven o'clock that night?
I was a morning baby my mum says,
the best kind. I was born
with my eyes open, you see?
Would you like to hear me sing?
I can almost dance, too.
Would you? I can hear
that she knows, Priam's daughter,
all her years to heaven –
that ever word was once
a poem, isn't it?

Takahe 35 (1998)

W. HART-SMITH (1911–1990)

No, I think a footsore sheep dog
obeying the weary whistle with a limp
or a close-up of gorse
lit with headlamps
leaning out all dusty at night
toward a brother thorn across the road;
or a stand of pine
lopped for firewood; yes, and a
solitary cabbage tree with its head blown off
a scraggy ruff of dead leaves
rattling at its neck. Not
these great chunks of landscape, Mount
Cook's fourteen guineas, rain on the
hills, south of this
and north of that. Please,
paint me a pub winder
with the din behind it.

Hand To Hand: A Garnering (Butterfly Books, 1991)

TRACTOR

Dragging an iron rake
the tractor wallows
across the ocean of the paddock
with a fine excitement of gulls
in its wake.

It has two large paddle wheels,
a funnel, with smoke;
and the captain is on the bridge.
Having cast off a couple
of moments ago,
he sets a course for the opposite hedge.

Hand To Hand: A Garnering (Butterfly Books, 1991)

H

DINAH HAWKEN (1943–)

1.

You're not ashamed of your past.
It hangs there in rust-coloured layers
and you curve out of it
fully at ease.

2.

Behind you the bay
sports expensive speed boats. More and more
they force their vibrations right up
your root-tips.

3.

You used to live here with other natives.
Now willows and poplars flickering gold
have proudly established themselves.

4.

I've heard you discussed as an item
of our international trade. They
conceive of you standing in each
pebble garden of suburban Los Angeles.

5.

The man at the back
has asked how much I care about you.
He says you impede his view.

6.

In the bush near here
you gather in tight bunches
your pasts hanging down and spreading
over the ground like soft mats.

I want to crawl under there.
I need to know what you're chatting about.

7.

Rowing out as usual
to the calmest part of the lake
I hear a chain-saw preening itself
and sense the spikes stiffening on your trunks.

8.

Once I saw you at a Marist Centre
stiff and brittle like an empty erection,
no fronds, no flow.
Mary was cramped into a grotto nearby
totally into pleasing God.

9.

I was just wondering whether
Christ had risen again this year or not
(Good Friday was April Fool's Day)
when I saw three fantails fooling around
in your fronds, in the rain.

10.

Under your dark arms
that night with no moon
I decided to let my life
climb up quietly
like the rata on your trunk.

11.

It leans so superbly
your long black trunk
perhaps it is frightening
the man at the back.

12.

Suddenly, in the city,
staked into a neat fence
you poke out your black tongue.
Keep coming and coming
back into my life.

It has no sound and is blue (Victoria University Press, 1987)

IMMIGRANT

We sat marooned in the blue gloom
of that hotel room, dazed
by weeks at sea, ballasted with doubt

The baby mewled in afternoon heat,
muzzing her eyes with small soft fists.
We ate malt biscuits, uncorked champagne

that was warm, flat, sour.
It was Saturday night, closed,
foreign and suddenly all a mistake

In a small hour, Kath began to bleed
the fall of a tiny comma of a child.
She was echoed away through strange streets

Sunrise, the landscape reared up, bush,
hill, rock, quite still, and repeated
over and over and over and over

between me and the numb antarctic.

Night Kitchen (Mallinson Rendel, 1985)

JEFFREY PAPAROA HOLMAN

I lost him the first time
before I could grasp
who he was, what he did, where
he fitted with her

and it's always seemed so dumb:
how to lose something
as big as a father.

I lost him the next time
to the rum-running Navy
who took him and took him
and kept right on taking

and it wasn't my mistake
losing a vessel
as big as a father.

I lost him a third time
to a ship in a bottle
that rocked him and rocked him
and shook out his pockets

and no kind of magic
could slip me inside
with my father.

I lost him at home
when floorboards subsided
as he said and she said
went this way and that way

and dead in the water
I couldn't hang on
to my father.

The last time I lost him
I lost him for good:
the night and the day
the breath he was breathing

and death's head torpedoes
blew out of the water
the skiff of my father.

LOOK

As I arrange slim
stemmed flowers
at the ikebana class

one petal falls
and floats blue
upon the water.

It is then I remember
the agapanthus you
planted by the pond

they will be pale green now
and you will look each day
for the first colour.

You will say
– You should see my agapanthus
today – Just that.

And as this petal turns a deeper blue
I would say
– Look – Just that.

Natsukashii (Pemmican Press, 1998)

WINESONG 15

I will sing a lovesong
– do not hide your ears
it is time for heartsongs and it is time for tears –
lady, I am a lover
lady, I am a thief
and I need your heart, love
as I need wine and tide and beach –

I will sing a tidesong
to while away your fears
you will hear the sea sound, you will hear deep prayers
but lady, I am a loner
and truly, I am a thief
and I will keep your heart-love
within my bottle's reach

and take it out in moonlight
and finger it with awe
until mazed with night caresses
I'll praise the bottle more.

When I sing this winesong
you'd better stop your ears
it only brings you emptiness
and strange and hopeless cares –

Strands (Auckland University Press, 1992)

THE WINE-RICH ARTERIES

The rain is falling in my head
it lilts the rhythm of the dead
                    haere haere ki te po
the rain is falling in my heart

the sun is shining in my mind
it blinds the memories that I find
                    haere haere ki te po
the sun is burning up my heart.

the wind is blowing in my bones
it tries to dry the sap to stone
                    haere haere ki te po
            it seeks the wine-rich arteries
            all the sweet and pulsing parts
            all the debris of my heart
and whines to set them free:
whistle, wind, for futility
                    haere haere ki te po.

Strands (Auckland University Press, 1992)

PLEA BEFORE STORM

Like the sky-high seagulls
tossed from those thundering black
boulders of the clouds, you are
girl, setting off back home,
looking for the things you've lost –
a mislaid purse and raincoat,
wondering where you put them last;
and nearly ready now to climb
the cliffpath, trying to recall
the home you left for this,
what way you came.

The macrocarpa blackness
quickens; pine-belts black on the hills.

Storm is coming in that crazed
rustle of leaves, the frenzied
laughter of the seagulls skidding
spread-eagled on the light. Like ice
setting, the light sets hard.

It is coming fast. Lightning
and thunder quicken. No pause.

I'm sorry, forget what I said.
Come back inside.

Collected Poems (Penguin, 1980)

TOMORROW, SOUTH, LOVE, YES

The taupata at my door
plays host to visitors; nods
sagely to a passing breeze;
bows low, so low, announcing
entry to a heavy wind.

These winds have travelled many
miles of sea coast from the north.
At Bottle Creek they ease off,
often stay the night. I could
make comparisons I guess.

I won't. Instead to say how
good it is to see you, you
young thing, lady, passing through.
Tomorrow, south, love, yes. The
taupata is dancing too.

Collected Poems (Penguin, 1980)

ANA GATHERING CONES ON BATTLE HILL

When I do not know of what
to sing or speak – what tune,
what word – I watch and wait
the slow rising of the moon:

the moon so slowly rising,
a man can only wait
and watch and maybe sing
songs, speak words, of love or hate.

The moon last night in storm.
I watched it rage above
Battle Hill until the dawn.
That song was one of love.

Up there today among those
pines, we could, you thought, have been
aboard some ship in wild seas,
creaking jib, rib and beam.

I know of the many moons,
the shadows and the phases.
I know of as many women,
sung them silver phrases:

a moon for the river,
another for the sea.
This moon, tangled as ever.
You, of these dark trees to me.

Collected Poems (Penguin, 1980)

ROBIN HYDE (1906–1939)

I'd like to forget now, just for the one clear minute,
Or more, if my querulous heart would let me be,
Life and everything in it
Save this. Once on a day, under a crab-apple tree
Stood an old white horse with a velvety Roman nose,
And a child reached up to pat him – ah, warily! –
Since lately she'd met with a rose
Of damask petals, and fiercely indignant bee.
But the old white horse *liked* apples. He stood as still,
Munching them there, as the shadows brushed on the hill
In glades of amber and purple. The faint wet tang
Of macrocarpa leaves crept into her heart.
There was the world, apart
From all but an old white horse, a child, and a thrush that sang;
It might have been something of Schumann's; the child didn't know –
Far happier so.
There was no harm in that – in stroking a velvety nose,
Hearing the crunch of apples, looking at leaves in the lane.
No clever, treacherous torture, to work in the brain –
Everything simple and plain,
A bright-edged beautiful peace, that loves you and goes –
Lie quiet. Perhaps, if you're still, it may come again.

Persephone in Winter (Hurst & Blackett, 1937)

THE LAST ONES

But the last black horse of all
Stood munching the green-bud wind,
And the last of the raupo huts
Let down its light behind.
Sullen and shadow-clipped
He tugged at the evening star,
New-mown silver swished like straw
Over the manuka.
As for the hut, it said
No word but its meagre light,
Its people slept as the dead,
Bedded in Maori night.
'And there is the world's last door,
And the last world's horse,' sang the wind,
'With little enough before,
And what you have seen behind.'

Houses by the Sea (Caxton Press, 1952)

SISTERS

In a dream not long sped,
I stood on the sands, in the glassy-shattering reach of the waves,
Quarrelling with my sister,
And caught her arm, as in their first furious childish quarrel
Cain caught at Abel's sleeve.
Then I felt how thin her wrist was – thin as a young child's wrist,
Hardly more than the bones of the snowy alighting birds,
Or the mast of a boy's blue boat;
So slight the garment of flesh, thin the bone beneath,
Evanescent her young mortality.
But before I could see her eyes or speak her name,
The wave broke, covering all,
Brightening, enlarging the rock-pools.

Houses by the Sea (Caxton Press, 1952)

STRIKING A POSE

we'll stock up books
and wine and pie
then stop the clocks
and never die

we'll nail the windows
brick up the door
and live on a mattress
on the floor

if death still comes
we'll strike a pose
and hold our breath
until he goes

Educating the Body (Caxton Press, 1967)

A SHRINKING WORLD

how could I have thought
that One Tree Hill was a mountain
of lanky frizzy pines?

this morning it is a sandcastle
with a single gull's feather
tilting at the top

Rangitoto just yesterday
seemed a mile high
and stretched right across the sea

now it is near enough
to throw stones at
and small enough to miss

water must have got into the earth
and everything has shrunk –
I cannot get through my door

the walls of my room
lean on my shoulders
and the ceiling presses my head sideways

cries from the street have become faint
and reedy – air must be escaping
through a puncture in the sky

and love which had all the time
in the world only moments ago
has dwindled away into the centuries

The Dangers of Art (Cicada Press, 1980)

MURUROA: THE NAME OF THE PLACE

It is only a small island
but a name sticks to it
with as many syllables

as a continent. Names
have nothing to do with size,
they are tags to remind us

of the shape of the world.
It is dangerous to forget them.
We cannot retrace our lives

and our long voyagings
without words to light up
maps in the brain,

though sometimes names
may also echo the sound of a place,
catch the graunch of a glacier,

the wind that sucks up
the sands of a desert,
or the slow rumble of tropical seas.

Names radiate energy.
They give tongue to triumphs,
pleasures, desolations.

They may taste of syrup
or salt. They can lie to us
or cast stones. The syllables

may even suggest
split fragments of meanings.
They can trigger reactions

that detonate beneath oceans
of memory, then crumble away,
falling in on themselves, leaving

only their corruptions eating
into the reefs below the waves.
Names can break bones.

Anzac Day. Selected Poems (Hazard Press, 1997)

for Jenny

The lady walks in white.
Her love was   bellbirds
                              in the blood
ringing over the moon. Marlborough
that time walking through night   brightness
bush fragrant and silver   water calm
in the haunted place   where old lives
launch themselves into the light
off a cliff.   Her love was
needles in the nerves   flashing
and after, in the trees bent away
from a wind that didn't exist we heard
the spring   singing to itself.

                                        Mist
has turned the landscape   into a chinese print,
a few   tree-strokes and a hill-line,
the inlet pencilled with reeds, a chalk-face
sketched with cracks.   In bed
while an aberrant disc jockey   exiled
in the air after midnight
                              spins
through my head
                    the lady walks in white.

Triptych (Hazard Press, 1988)

J

MICHAEL JACKSON (1940–)

When this bruised medallion, the moon,
rose tonight
I thought how solitude
allows what human kind cannot –
openness to this hill whose eucalypts
are my hands,
the sky
which has seen me drown.

I float up
through these leaves, my skin,
breathing this blue again;
the moon
hangs round my neck,
under me men move to harvest
or lie against a golden stook
eating black bread
drinking red wine.

The moon is the pupil of my eye
I go as far as the blue hill goes
I flow like a river in the dark.

Going On (John McIndoe, 1985)

SEVEN MYSTERIES

Now write down
the seven mysteries:
why you so young and beautiful should die;
why consciousness prevents
escape into the chestnut branches where
foliage goes soft
with God's vermilion;
why what is said is seldom what was meant;
why men and women work, come home,
cook meals, argue and renew
their vows of silence or revenge;
why we were different;
why there are seven of everything;
why I go on
broken-winded like that horse we saw
on the ridge above Waipatiki
by a bent tree
watching the waves roll in.

Going On (John McIndoe, 1985)

J

HELEN JACOBS (1929–)

I think it will be easy soon
to slip out of my skin –

you have already practised
making me into a photograph –

you are more at ease
without my voice –

i am seldom the flesh
at your side –

you can fill the rooms
with your isolation –

there. Five jerks
and I have metamorphosed
into an idea inside my own head.
I left the house tidy for you.

The Usefulness of Singing (Sudden Valley Press, 1999)

THE BEARER

It never was the custom
for women to carry the coffin.

Once they would have walked behind,
black-veiled under the hot sun,
weeping, perhaps chanting the words
to send the soul, while the men, silent
and steel-faced, stiffly marched the body
into the grave.

But, today,
in the way the woman feels the baby
pulling down on the weight of the breast,
in the way the mother holds the child's
heaviness on her shoulder,
in the way she steadies the child-adult
leaning uncertainly from her,
in the way she bears the weight of the man
pressing upon her, supports the slow weariness
of the head, then the failing body,

in just that way, today,
you carried the coffin.

How Things Are (Whitireia Publishing and Daphne Brasell Ass.,
1996)

LOUIS JOHNSON (1924–1988)

I praise Saint Everyman, his house and home
In every paint-bright gardened suburb shining
With all the age's verities and welcome
Medalled upon him in contentment dining;
And toast with gin and bitters
The Muse of baby-sitters.

I sing Dame Everyone's whose milky breast
Suckles the neighbourhood with pins and plans
Adding new rooms to their eternal rest,
The next night's meat already in the pan:
And toast with whisky and ice,
The Goddess who keeps things nice.

I honour Maid Anybody's whose dreams are shaping
Lusts in her heart down the teasing garden-path
Where she stops in time as she must at the gaping
Graveyard of Hell and rescues her girlish laugh:
And toast in rum and cloves
The course of balanced *love.*

I drink to Son Mostpeople's whose honourable pride
In things being what they are will not let him run,
But who keeps things going even after he has died
In a distant desert clutching an empty gun:
And toast in brandy and lime
The defenders of our great good time.

New Worlds for Old (Capricorn Press, 1957)

The hotels are quieter this year: the merest
peppering at the tables tonight, and all of them
eating alone. They do not look about or wish
to talk. A finger stabs the menu: a pencil
records with the faint whisper of grass
in a small breeze. Behind the palms
a faceless music registers dismay from its can
as neutrally as maybe. In the lounge
the news has the air of having been suppressed
and is as quickly forgotten. And so
to bed. There will be nothing here
for the diary entry. A cigarette in the dark
ripens its one dangerous fruit.

Winter Apples (Mallinson Rendel, 1984)

DEPARTURES

You come away from here
with the feeling of having lost,
yet scarcely aware of the sense
of having arrived. Everything so swift
nothing at all seemed to happen but
a few fast impressions. The girl
shaking a mat from the balcony:
dogs below, getting on with it;
the menu exposing itself at the café door.

And something fixed in the way
the sun stood at noon. A red
geranium bloomed in a big pot
and a snake shivered across
the flagstones. Everything suddenly
seemed to go underground at the point
of awakening. Where shall you go
now? It all seems darker:
the road fading out, without trace.

Last Poems (Antipodes Press, 1990)

TREASURE HUNT 7

Be glad there's still a morepork or two left
to make the night eerie – standing in the kitchen, hands slick
with soapy water, I look out the window
as one of these shy owls lands on a manuka branch
and stares in at me with her big, brown
unblinking eyes. I ask, 'What are you doing, bird,
out and about before twilight. And you must know
this is the Kingdom of Claws.'

'I am here with a message,'
the bird says, 'I carry an omen on my wings.'
'What is it?' I ask, quickly drying my hands.
'Just this,' says the bird and flies away.

You must find the bird. You must
lower yourself into the disillusioned depths of her prescient eyes,
you must hold her in your hands without claws

            you must lift her sleeping wings
and read

            in the feathered pattern of moon and cloud
the riddle of her flight.

Treasure Hunt (Auckland University Press, 1996)

MIKE JOHNSON (1947–)

ANDREW JOHNSTON (1963–)

FOR ROSE

Rosie Marsland, b 26/7/94

What does sunlight sound like?
A white flower in darkness knows,

an ear that hears both ways, and sees –
sirens, and silence; laughter, and after;

conversation of insects all over the house
and a steady heart

thinking *the the the*
and Rose's ear, born furled, unfolds

that hears these, and those, and knows –
Rose listens to the world, the world listens to Rose.

The Sounds (Victoria University Press, 1996)

BOAT

A boat though no more than a thought
might carry us, far from

the coast, as far as
we know. But

is it a ship then,
cresting and sounding? I think,

for its boasting, it's just a boat
drifting down a difficult river –

now and then it runs aground
and that is where we live.

The Sounds (Victoria University Press, 1996)

J

M.K. JOSEPH (1914–1981)

I cannot give
   Unless I have
I cannot have
   Unless I save
Unless I have
   I cannot save
Unless I give
   I cannot have.

Unless I live
   I cannot be
Unless I am
   I cannot seem
I cannot be
   Unless I seem
I cannot live
   Unless I am.

I cannot be
   Unless I give
I cannot have
   Unless I die
Unless I grieve
   I cannot love
Unless I die
   I cannot live.

Inscription on a Paper Dart: Selected Poems 1945–72 (Auckland
University Press/Oxford University Press, 1974)

WAITING AT THE STATION

When's the train coming, mum?
    Will it be soon?
– The man said to wait, dear,
    Till the afternoon.

But I'm tired of waiting
    Let's go home again.
– We have to wait, dear,
    We might miss the train.

When's dad coming back, mum?
    When'll we see dad?
– After a long journey
    My little lad.

What are the soldiers doing
    By the trucks over there?
– They're going to the beach, dear,
    For some nice fresh air.

Can't we go with them
    Can't we go away?
– Perhaps you will, little man,
    Some day, some day.

I'm tired, mum, tired,
    Take me home to bed.
– I'll spread the rug on the suitcase
    So lie down, sleepyhead.

I can hear the pistons thumping
    And the whistles calling.
– The trains have all gone, dear,
    Those are bombs falling.

Inscription on a Paper Dart: Selected Poems 1945–72 (Auckland
University Press/Oxford University Press, 1974)

DRUNKEN GUNNERS

The gunners move like figures in a dance
Harmoniously at their machine that kills
Quite casually beyond the shadowed hills
Under the blue and echoing air of France.
The passing driver watches them askance:
'Look at the beggars – pickled to the gills.'
Yet bodies steadied in parade-ground skills
Correct the tottering mind's intemperance.

Housed under summer leafage at his ease,
Artillery board set up, the captain sees
His rule connect two dots a league apart
And throws destruction at hypotheses,
Wishing that love had ministers like these
To strike its distant enemy to the heart.

Inscription on a Paper Dart: Selected Poems 1945–72 (Auckland
University Press/Oxford University Press, 1974)

SECURITY

from THE IMMIGRANT CYCLE

After the long day
my father locks the doors,
the windows, the blinds on the windows,
he locks out the voice of the wind,
the question
of yesterday
whatisit whatisit whatisit

My mother turns off every light
in every room, in every cupboard,
she turns off the TV,
the red light of the heart flashing
whatisit whatisit
the last star
in this forever foreign sky

And carefully they lie in bed listening
to the sound of growing children.

All roads lead to the sea (Auckland University Press, 1997)

Port-Vila, New Hebrides '74

Beneath the liveries of day
lives a nightly cat
black beast
who prowls at stroke of three.

My sometime me
the late late show
when I miss
the innocent call to sleep.

She unlike the daytime self
wears sharper spectacles
no rose-tints. Her coat
sheens against the night
her stockings are seamed
a purple band winds round her hat
no sweet song lines her throat.

She strides the decks
some Lucifress to the night
she haunts stars fallen in the sea.
The moon lopes an ocean of cloud
ropes flack the mast
a bat comes sliding.

At four, peacocks cut the air
with scabbed voices.

Who is there here
but this sounding air
this dark this phosphorous
I splash from the sea?

She waits for that strike of furious light
a comet across her sky.

Against the Softness of Woman (Caveman Press, 1976)

PACT FOR MOTHER AND TEENAGER

Girl, we've quarrelled
in a motel in a strange town.
It's 2 a.m. and tomorrow
I'm due to drive north all day
on the holiday we've planned
this six months past.
If you were a lover,
I'd have thrown you out;
if you were your father,
I might have had a bitter-sweet
reconciliation. But as you are
my child, I watch you sleep
tangled in bedsheets and tearstains,
and try to plan the shortest way
out of town.

Wakeful Nights (Vintage, 1991)

ANZAC '77

A sequel to Guy Fawkes '58

The celebrations are both of fire
and equal exercises in futility,
exploding stars or bleeding
heart poppies,

we of the grey generation
might have learnt something,
or so we would think, yet
as I said my goodbyes
nearly twenty years ago
beneath a sky of falling rockets,
how could I imagine that this morning,
with last posts tootling ghostly nonsense
everywhere, I would hear a boy's name
on the radio, killed in a brawl,
I was sure it was your son.

He could have been ours,
but that was long ago,
I bear no rancour,
love has honed many a sharp new edge
since then, and right now,
all I can honestly recall
of you,
is a quiet (unseemly then) capacity
for grief.

The summer's last carnations bleed
on my window ledge. Across the years
I stretch my hands, cup them briefly,
expecting to hold your bursting heart,
and rightly for such presumption,
find them empty:

the fires rain down, each generation
determines some obscene new absurdity
to maintain its rituals.
We did no better,
and all our stars were hollow.

Wakeful Nights (Vintage, 1991)

LEONARD LAMBERT (1945 –)

Dogs bark
   and the low valley stirs
      to hollow dogs of the hills
         the long water years

a black cloud covers the sun
   the warm wind at my back
      bristles the gorse
         sniffs at my neck.

down the wires
   someone calls and calls
      and I feel them rise
         ghostly run

from oilskin hills
   beds of stone
      all those long-gone laddies
         loping home.

A Washday Romance (John McIndoe, 1980)

SOMEWHERE IN AUGUST

When the sea comes pouring through the town
Faded signs revive, boarding houses bloom;
Warring down-at-heel couples call it a day,
Old Barry peeps through semi-sober eyes,
Half-decides to flag it away.

A low background roar swallows jackhammer and drill,
Cloudy workers whistle and call –
Twenty feet today is a dizzy height –
Dalliance and Beau fill the slow easy air,
Follow winterclad women in the softening light.

With a low-running sea almost blue
And the salt thick on windscreen and window,
Freighting a steady breeze, a mariner's wind,
On a certain Friday somewhere in August
Spring of all things comes urging inland.

That high-rolling summer that sweeps
Through the suburbs like Lotto, that raps
And bangs up and down the land, demanding Play –
That's another world, a big loud bugger
More than half a year away –

But the body knows and the whole town can feel,
Despite the forecast rain the chill
And the sun only weakly shining,
Out beyond the bare-masted trees
Somewhere some tide is turning.

Park Island (John McIndoe, 1990)

MICHELE LEGGOTT (1956–)

from **A WOMAN, A ROSE, AND WHAT HAS IT TO DO WITH HER OR THEY WITH ONE ANOTHER?**

1

Do you see me? I am falling out of a blue sky where my days were
as dancers in a maze, sure-footed and smiling. I stood in my
garden pulling loquats off the tree and eating them to be full of
spring. I filled up on summer and kept the city busy with
correspondence. Flightpaths criss-crossed at my feet, bees fizzed
and joy was my middle name.

Then a pair of taxis went head to head in a distant country so
suddenly I didn't see the difference but it was a wide white
threshold. When I couldn't thread a needle, when I could no
longer see the faces of my children or trim their nails, when the
colour of money disappeared (and I bareheaded in the midday
sun) then falling began and I cried out against it. What's one wing
beating time on the steel drum of the sky? What is the sight of my
eyes to the great oratory of the labyrinth?

There was a send-off, they gave me flowers and asked where I
would go. To open the eyes of the soul, I said. Good wishes
hovered over the gathering and messages flew into my pockets.
There is a way, I said, but this is only the first gate. I give what is
left of the light of my eyes, I have fallen out of a clear sky.

As far as I can see (Auckland University Press, 1999)

THE ENTRANCE TO PURGATORY

What you will notice first is the air's
greater clarity: you had not remembered
how it gave to trees the instructive simplicity
of a botanist's drawing. The hills too, so distant
but so sharply delineated, seeming to wait
for a turret, a temple, a whole town
circumscribed by justice: in the foreground a space
left for Madonna and Infant, and in the southern sky
new stars hanging as beacons of virtue.

You are glad to be here, when it would have been so easy
at the last moment simply to permit
the past its habitual choice: blind, heavy-handed
and hopeless in its passion. Even so
that you are here, that you are no longer hunting
an imaginary shape through streets of lead
turning back always upon the same dead vista
of northern cities which have lost their hearts for ever
seems mere chance, although it is not.

For the light which bathes these streets is sober, the sun
though welcoming as love is placed to illuminate
an architecture whose details always tell
the same legend. Those whiskered bigots who planned
this city in holy ignorance of its terrain
meant it a cradle of virtue, but perhaps you must
return here more than once, your suitcase crammed
with disappointments and leading loss by the hand
to learn how insistently its ways will bring

you always to one point, until their choice becomes
your second nature. But this is only the beginning
when suffering seems a new adventure, the past
a backdrop lending it dignity. Later you must unpack
pictures and broken ornaments, making them

the measure of your loss, and what it takes to forgive.
Here too the city will help, hill tree and tower
by sunlight or by starlight assembled into a setting
for something to take place in, a place to go on from.

The Entrance to Purgatory (John McIndoe, 1986)

MY TOASTER TELLS THE TIME

One side: time
to read (if you're quick) four
sonnets or intone
one penitential psalm   time
to make a shopping list and feel
a cold or a poem coming on or run
into the great hall of memory and out
again   oh time
to know quite certainly you're
no longer loved that time
is a trickster   time
to fall down dead
and leave time
to grow black and burn
the house with its great hall
its poems lists and lovers that made
the shape and stuff of time.

Winter Walk at Morning (Victoria University Press, 1991)

RACHEL McALPINE (1940–)

Well to get to the nitty-gritty,
here it is:
I was suddenly sick of praying
to men, for men.
That was the beginning,
the middle and the end.

Ritual: remind myself I am guilty,
wrong, and light in the head.

Orthodox theology and common sense:
yes our Father is sexless,
God is being, God is love,
yes the Holy Spirit is spirit
and Jesus being a Jew
simply had to be male
and he was kind to girls.
Yes I could alter pronouns privately,
yes I am married to God
and have no right to divorce.
Yes Man is metaphor for Woman,
yes I could work within,
yes I could wait a century
yes it is just as silly
to think of God as Woman –

yet things are right for me
when flesh and spirit agree:
I do not feel included.

One truth is that God the Father
calls mostly to men except
when he wants a cup of tea.

Selected Poems (Mallinson Rendel, 1988)

HOUSE PROUD

from HOUSE POEMS

she isn't easy to befriend
rancid and set in her tricks
Who me? she says Let me rot
along with my pirate tom-cats

she pleads arthritis too
displays her wretched joints and swellings
and skin as thin as water
I am winsome and considerate

showdown: no more whining
to put it bluntly
the house hurls blanks
wall after wall all eight by ten

I tremble and drink brandy but
grovelling is over
there is and there isn't a haven
once you have run to the cave

hovel, I punish, reward and heal you
with gib board, paper and paint

Selected Poems (Mallinson Rendel, 1988)

JOY MACKENZIE

A sign in the park
says beware
of the magpies

We walk under tall trees
The magpies scold and gossip
It's cold and we don't know

where we're going
The trees don't tell
mynahs and magpies

to get out of their space
One day we say
we're going to learn

the names of these trees
You try to dress me
in your past

lover's black scarf
I am twisting and turning
and watching

the magpies
There's danger ahead
I won't wear it

Sport 20 (Autumn 1998)

THE ROOM

for Kate and Bruce

I want to photograph this room
which isn't mine. Not the usual snap
of children, tree and presents, but
light on the pages
of 'Hark the Herald Angels Sing'
and the keys of the cranky piano, left
by someone off overseas. I'd show
the big blue armchairs
crouching in shadow
like patient animals, and nut-coloured
panelling, nearly to the ceiling. These walls
were built by people
who kept families sealed
and secure, the way
I felt sealed in my childhood
and longed to escape.
Finally, I'd frame the view
out the front window. At midday
the lawn glitters in the sun
and children fall through time
so quickly, no one can catch them.

The Inland Eye (Pemmican Press, 1998)

M

CILLA McQUEEN (1949–)

TIMEPIECE

I got home from work and looked at
my watch and it said
Ten to five, so I did the washing and
picked some greens and tidied up the
kitchen and sat down and had a cup of coffee,
and looked at my watch and still it said
Ten to five, so I did some ironing and
made the beds and thought Hell I might
get all the housework done in one day
for a change, then looked at my watch
but nope, no change, and I turned on the
radio and it said Ten to five, so
I cleaned the bathroom like mad and
picked some flowers and wrote some
letters and some cheques and scrubbed
the kitchen floor and got started on the
windows – by this time I was getting a bit
desperate I can tell you, I was thinking
alternately Yay! soon there'll be no more to
do and I'll be free, and Jeez what if I
RUN OUT? I did in fact run out, and out,
and out, past the church clock saying
Ten to five and the cat on the corner with
big green eyes ticking away, and up into the
sky past the telephone wires, and
up into the blue, watchless, matchless, timeless
cloud-curtains, where I hide, and
it is silent, silent.

Homing In (John McIndoe, 1982)

Here again.
Dark's falling. Stand
on the corner of the verandah
in the glass cold clear
night, looking out
to emerald and ruby harbour
lights:
        too sharp to stay
out long,
        enough just to
greet the bones lying
on the moon
and two fishing boats
homing in.

Homing In (John McIndoe, 1982)

QUARK DANCE

here come the colours
to settle on our lips and eyes
and rainbow lighting all the edges
the boundaries are unstable
trust love not logic
light falls
never the same way twice
keep awake
jump out into the never-look-back
I can if you can too
barefoot balance and free fall
without scary death in our mouths
just plain delight
learning to nudge the wind
dance falling exploding symmetry
stretching the space
pulse slow arm elbow up
whip spine twist
thigh knee toe out
the current passes
nowadays science is pure poetry
all the particles bounce and decay
sweetly and sure as seeds
and quarks come in such colours and flavours
as beauty charm and strangeness
it's all so weird and simple
the world's made up of tiny little energetic
multicoloured irrational jellybeans
so dance
quark dance

anti gravity (John McIndoe, 1984)

PATRICK

Nine years have passed
since that telephone call.

This afternoon we walk past
the tree we planted over your ashes.

Your mother admires
a chaffinch landing cheekily
beside us on the duck pond rail.

We stroll up to the swings
where she says if you were alive now
she wouldn't remember you playing there

nor would I describe a chaffinch,
chestnut, confident, elegant, commanding
attention by its very presence alongside us.

Pingandy: New & Selected Poems (HeadworX, 1999)

MAKESHIFT HOLDING PEN

from YESTERDAY

My grandfather possessed
places with great names,
Omana,
the big house
overlooking the railyards,
Rocky Peak,
a view of almost
all of Banks Peninsula,
Western Valley,
a quiet creek,
dragonflies & native bees.

He seemed to spend his time
shifting sheep between the three.

Any excuse to practise the dogs
for those heroic winter days
when he would stride out to
the circle & with whistle, shout
& stick, control all brute creation.

Pingandy: New & Selected Poems (HeadworX, 1999)

THE SONG

My body as an act of derision,
eating up the answers to life.
There is the bird-song, now,
elbowing through berries while
the hairs in my nose catch
at the little bits of existence.

And I know you go on living
because you need to be cared for.
I embrace you, I kiss you,
trusting in an ordered development,
watching the small explosions
under your wrists.

Oh we survive merely by good fortune,
by random appetite: going
outside to lie on our stomachs
as if we meant to swim in the earth,
floating near the dazed horizon,
giving this music into the light.

How to Take Off Your Clothes at the Picnic (Wai-te-ata Press, 1977)

POEM FOR VANESSA

1

She wants to fly
Like a big flower floating
Like clouds above the house

She wants to sing at breakfast
She won't eat toast
She wants to catch my eye

And I am writing her
The longest poem in the Southern Hemisphere!
Oh passages of cloud & sky!

2

The longest poem in the Southern Hemisphere
Regrettably, has little to say
About the Southern Hemisphere

We know that the people
Are small and dark
Dark hair, dark eyes

We know they live in dreams along the coast
They make their small dark noises
And they cry

3

Oh who am I talking to?
That is, to whom am I talking?
Oh, not to you

And not to you:
The longest poem in the Southern Hemisphere
Alas, is not for every eye

Subsequent sections
Shall go directly
To Vanessa, by and by

Good Looks (Auckland University Press/Oxford University Press, 1982)

ANTARCTIC STONE

in my hand
and the spine of a hill
inside the stone

dark ridge of earth & bone
then inclines and heights
and sudden drops

where whatever pours
is wind, is ice, forgetting itself
at last in light

in quiet line, horizon

What to Call Your Child (Godwit, 1999)

Last night for the first time since you were dead
I walked with you, my brother, in a dream.
We were at home again beside the stream
Fringed with tall berry bushes, white and red.
'Don't touch them: they are poisonous,' I said.
But your hand hovered, and I saw a beam
Of strange bright laughter flying round your head
And as you stooped I saw the berries gleam –
'Don't you remember? We called them Dead Man's Bread!'
I woke and heard the wind moan and the roar
Of the dark water tumbling on the shore.
Where – where is the path of my dream for my eager feet?
By the remembered stream my brother stands
Waiting for me with berries in his hands . . .
'These are my body. Sister, take and eat.'

Poems of Katherine Mansfield (Oxford University Press, 1988)

THE MAN WITH THE WOODEN LEG

There was a man lived quite near us;
He had a wooden leg and a goldfinch in a green cage.
His name was Farkey Anderson,
And he'd been in a war to get his leg.
We were very sad about him,
Because he had such a beautiful smile
And was such a big man to live in a very small house.
When he walked on the road his leg did not matter so much;
But when he walked in his little house
It made an ugly noise.
Little Brother said his goldfinch sang the loudest of all birds,
So that he should not hear his poor leg
And feel too sorry about it.

Poems of Katherine Mansfield (Oxford University Press, 1988)

LATTER-DAY GEOGRAPHY LESSON

This, quoth the Eskimo master
　　was London in English times:
　　step out a little faster
　　you two young men at the last there
　　the Bridge would be on our right hand
　　and the Tower near where those crows stand –
　　we struck it you'll recall in Gray's rhymes:
　　this, quoth the Eskimo master
　　was London in English times.

This, quoth the Eskimo master
　　was London in English days:
　　beyond that hill they called Clapham
　　boys that swear Master Redtooth I slap 'em
　　I dis-tinct-ly heard-you-say-Bastard
　　don't argue: here boys, ere disaster
　　overtook her, in splendour there lay
　　a city held empires in sway
　　and filled all the earth with her praise:
　　this quoth the Eskimo master
　　was London in English days.

She held, quoth the Eskimo master
　　ten million when her prime was full
　　from here once Britannia cast her
　　gaze over an Empire vaster
　　even than ours: look there Woking
　　stood, I make out, and the Abbey
　　lies here under our feet *you great babby*
　　Swift-and-short do-please-kindly-stop-poking
　　your thumbs through the eyes of that skull.

Collected Poems (Victoria University Press, 1990)

ON THE SWAG

His body doubled
    under the pack
    that sprawls untidily
    on his old back
    the cold wet dead-beat
    plods up the track.

The cook peers out :
    'oh curse that old lag –
    here again
    with his clumsy swag
    made of a dirty old
    turnip bag.'

'Bring him in cook
    from the grey level sleet
    put silk on his body
    slippers on his feet,
    give him fire
    and bread and meat.

Let the fruit be plucked
    and the cake be iced,
    the bed be snug
    and the wine be spiced
    in the old cove's night-cap:
    for this is Christ.'

Collected Poems (Victoria University Press, 1990)

Judas Iscariot
  sat in the upper
  room with the others
  at the last supper

And sitting there smiled
  up at his master
  whom he knew the morrow
  would roll in disaster.

At Christ's look he guffawed –
  for then as thereafter
  Judas was greatly
  given to laughter,

Indeed they always said
  that he was the veriest
  prince of good fellows
  and the whitest and merriest.

All the days of his life
  he lived gay as a cricket
  and would sing like the thrush
  that sings in the thicket

He would sing like the thrush
  that sings on the thorn
  oh he was the most sporting bird
  that ever was born.

Collected Poems (Victoria University Press, 1990)

MIKE MINEHAN (1947–)

on the estuary the oyster catcher considers
journeys
smells spice on the antarctic air
gathers its feathers close
and practises deep breathing
crazy mutters helen
who'd want to go to siberia?

susan sculpting goddesses in her garden
under kites and totems
tilts her nose towards the sea
scents her lover in east riding
and files her nails
helen lights a candle
all this travelling she sighs
makes me itch

the land turns chill and snow creeps down the mountain
the river crackles to the sea
the women build fires
and warm their hands on each other
dreaming of pyramids
and sweet spices & lovers
helen smiles
in march, she whispers, we'll go to egypt.

Embracing the Dark (Hazard Press, 1991)

M

I came to the crest of Owairaka and turned about,
And my love was a cloud and this peak
Was a wave of the sea carrying me
Back to Kakepuku and to thee.
I would hold Pirongia as once you held me
Toko, my cousin and my love, this callow heart
Thought two nights together worth a lifetime apart.
Toa of the South, Mania of the West,
We were well met. I thought to rest
Forever in your arms, but was torn from your breast,
Dragged back to the land of my birth,
To the boiling pools and smouldering earth
That once warmed Ngatoroirangi, on the edge of death,
Saved by his sisters from Tongariro's cold breath;
Even Tongariro, in his great love,
Was granted the mountain Pihanga as wife.

But we whelped only wind and rain,
Begat storms of the West in our pain.

Maori Poetry: The Singing Word (Price Milburn for Victoria University Press, 1974)

Note: The original poem, written by Rihi Puhiwahine, was in Maori as WAIATA AROHA O NGA MAUNGA and has been translated by Barry Mitcalfe.

MICHAEL MORRISSEY (1942–)

slowly my imaginary grandmother
is running

out of real teeth
she never eats celery

never touches hard
mythologies

has no truck with old
man death

whom she says
is fresh out of

work allowing him
only to rake up

the leaves
put out the rubbish

and generally make
himself useful

every day she walks
her cat half a mile

to the park
sits on the seesaw

gives him the up
and down treatment

which she says is good
for his sinuses

really my imaginary
grandmother looks like

Lloyd George rules
a great empire

from her cottage
where she herbs

a harmless garden
of witchcraft

now and then
befriending aloof comets

which she knows how
to freeze

in the silent
moments

men call art

Landfall 167 (September 1988)

SHOES

ELIZABETH NANNESTAD (1956–)

from A PORTRAIT OF MY MOTHER
in her memory

Shoes, shoes, how Mother liked shoes
and hats and gloves and lacy stockings.
She always had. When she was very young, six or seven,
and her mother took her to buy shoes
she tried on every shoe in the shop
and sat in the centre
with them all around her in a circle.

Mother swore allegiance to the four inch heel.
Through thick and thin she was faithful.
She turned her nose up at the outdoors generally
but I do remember her once
walking along a beach in her heels.

My mother did not give in to the mere nature of things.
Not anyway to sand.

If He's A Good Dog He'll Swim (Auckland University Press, 1996)

HER VOICE

from A PORTRAIT OF MY MOTHER
in her memory

I would give anything to hear her now –
her voice hardened by experience,
grainy like some kind of not-too-sweet honey
that pours steadily.

It was like
in sickness, in any dark room shifting,
the warm cloth, that lies
not heavily.

Her laugh pushed trees down and split them.
In any little thing she said, even just Good Morning,
you could hear that she had been
to places without even stars
and come back to say,
There is nothing there worth taking seriously.

If He's A Good Dog He'll Swim (Auckland University Press, 1996)

PRESUMING THE WORST

So what if the dead did come back again?
Perhaps there wouldn't be fear, nor joy at first,
but angry accusations

like when I'd gone missing, though not for long
just cycled to the left of a divided road
after you'd gone right, and we met back at home –

you rammed your bicycle up against mine
cussed: 'For fuckssake I was worried
thought you could have been snatched, or hit by a truck,
I swear I'm sick of you, I've had about enough'

and when I reached out
to seek the kiss of your voltaic skin,
convinced our hands could easily unslip
the loose running-knot of such quick fury,

you ran your knuckles over your eyes
looked and stepped straight through me.

Sleeve-notes (Godwit, 1999)

You open the book
& there unfolds a road   its skin is blue, it is summer
the heat   that dances in its hollows turns

into water.   You ride it in the vehicles of strangers:
homesteads & haybarns   dusty yellow sheeptrucks
convoy of soldiers in jungle greens returning

from an exercise
slipping past their polarized windscreens;
you draw from them splinters   of lives made of words

though you never take your eyes off the mountains.
The mountains   reach out to embrace you
they fold their blue ankles

they give birth to rivers, they
can even crouch like tigers if that's the way you
want them: they are a story you tell

about yourself, a story you are journeying
into, which swallows you.   You leave
the road, then   you honour the logic of ridges

& gorges, of funnels, of slotted
stone chimneys   You startle a huge bird
nesting in the riverbed, climbing on slow

cream & ash coloured wings   & you follow
as it disappears
inland, you tunnel to the spine of the island

& bury yourself   alive, with your possessions, this
curved sky, this whisper of ice-cloud
this magic mountain slamming shut behind you.

The Listener (16 November 1985)

A LOVE SONG

Ngati Porou

Were you, beloved, to invite me,
Straightway, by way of the hill I would come
Lest I stray afar, and eagerly I would
Follow the path you trod.
Alas, you are gone, as if borne on high
By some magic enchantment.

Why did you not when first we met
Set about undoing our affection;
Before love had fastened firmly
And become a consuming desire?

Comes it now, I am a derelict canoe,
Stripped to the hull, alas.
Sink down, O sun, presently to set,
Come then copious tears.
False lips you have, thou descendant of Makiri,
Of whose infamy we have already heard!

Of you, dear one, no word is heard,
You are, as a father, quite lost.
Unlike, thou art, the waning moon which dies,
Later, is seen again on high.

Nga Moteatea, Part 1 (The Polynesian Society, 1959)

surprising everybody
and almost himself
he spun on his heel
and swung savagely
at the small bladder
which he knew with certainty
comprised parts of pig
and with a swift boot
made up he knew with
equal certainty
from parts of calf
he lifted the ex-pig
high into the sky
and sent it zinging
between two posts of ex-tree

whereupon the terraces
erupted with brays
bleats and exultant whinnies
and waved bits of sheep about
in the colourful air

The Sportsman & Other Poems (Hard Echo Press, 1987)

PARTIAL ECLIPSE

when the sky was smudged
with just the faintest
suggestion of brown bottle
I realized that this was
all we were going to get

despite all those seductive
rumours spreading
through the grass with
enough of an after-
slither a snakelike ripple
to frighten the children

despite the table set up
in the bright sunshine
the aneroid barometer
graph paper and exposed
black and white film

so I said sometimes
nothing is better than
almost nothing and
waited for the wind
and the birds to return

and the wind did
swirling heavy with rain
and the birds did
beating their wings
like the hearts of the children
whose staring faces stayed
deep in the shadows
of what might have been

A Kind of Kingdom (Victoria University Press, 1998)

Now Eugene is flying home
    for good, who could tell the hour
by aeroplanes crossing Saint
    Patrick's, a line of pills

along the dresser; who picked up
    the ghost of an early
spring morning and shook it
    this world a small weight

off his back. A windy day, I pinned
    my drawings to the floor, the eye
adrift with its horizons, tiny
    splinters of them – you might have

taught me that, Eugene, this life's
    little work, 'carry home
what you can', to die among
    indefinable rivers, trees

this far. I was seventeen
    feet tall at Piha Beach
surf lifted me that high
    I could see *life* and you just

beyond it, the four loud companions
    (you would call them 'saints')
beside your hospital bed, those four
    silent men. The road, Eugene,

is made of stone. I still
    cannot play the guitar. This
light you will bathe in
    coming close
                to that.

In memory, Eugene O'Sullivan, d. 1988, Ireland

Days Beside Water (Auckland University Press, 1993)

STORM WARNING

after Colin McCahon

If, cloud-laden, the weather teaches us
a windswept humility, our children teach us

a kind of responsibility to all that is not yet formed.
Beyond beacon and wind-turbine, the half-formed storm dictates

its warning. And while our blindness teaches us how to tell
a bombed out bridge (because our children in their wisdom

cannot) from a moonlit ridge, our mathematics suggests
storms have their structures too, and how the southerly

is responsible for more than a dim day's light, ice-trails,
the early delivery of children. But it is the distant percussion

of the inner ear, our deafness that will teach us and go on
teaching us until there is no blueness on the face

of the earth, that a storm warning is only once,
then all we are left with, the storm.

Winter I Was (Victoria University Press, 1999)

THANK YOU

my one appearance at
the parish dance
found me at first unsuccessful
with the ladies.
then I worked it out: the *imprimatur*
was to be seen talking
to the smiling priest who presided
by the stage. this done
I found a free one
who as it happened
was spending her last
week of secularity before
joining the noviciate.
'*thank you.*'
toward the end
I persuaded another to let me
drive her home.
this, it transpired,
meant *drive her home:* her manner
was clerical, but inclusive:
'thank you fellow parishioner,'
the car door slammed.
above the trees
a ball moon that appeared
to ache & suggest
something unattainable about love.

A Particular Context (Sudden Valley Press, 1999)

THE ROTARY WASHER

my mother
was much devoted
to the Virgin Mary.

men (including the Good Lord)
had their uses to be sure
but mainly

of the out-of-doors sort –
digging potatoes, painting the wooden butterfly,
chopping down trees.

women, on the other hand,
'understood'. that's where
Mary came in: blue, benevolent,

predictable as plaster.
when the nuns
wanted a rotary washer

they asked
my mother to first soften the monseigneur's
heart toward them . . .

this she did, but not
without the intercession of the Blessed Virgin –
after all, she *knew* about washing.

A Particular Context (Sudden Valley Press, 1999)

PEACOCKS

Strangely in this suburb peacocks constantly cry
strutting behind their wire. If there were tended
lawns sloping to a docile river, if an antique
decorum was defined when the birds shrieked
and displayed flamboyant sexual colours to the eyes
of gentlepeople pacing gravelled paths
who in such ways were minded of the other
uses for the languorous summer half-light . . .
no mullioned windows mask unambiguous ardours
discreetly managed behind closed curtains.
Still, the birds shriek and exhibit the colours
of appetite and desire; within the weatherboard houses
there's passion enough. Though the decorum has departed
the curtains are strictly drawn and the nights are close.

Out of Season (Oxford University Press, 1980)

My father's bomber
jacket still hangs on
a peg beside a squadron photo.
Once I tried it on
but found that it was
far too small.
After all
when he wore it
he was not much more
than a boy –
in his tin machine
with his instruments
and weapons
alone and
far from
land
way out above the Pacific
as the waves beneath
moved like cards
being shuffled.

Breeze (Auckland University Press, 1991)

CONTAINER TERMINAL

The sun rising
above Rangitoto . . .
there were tracks
across the tide
I stood in sunlight
the colour of containers.
An old freighter with
a beard of rust
lay anchored
in midstream.
Gulls flew between
the masts of moored ships.
Huge wharf cranes
walked the water's edge.
Into my hand they lowered an island.

Breeze (Auckland University Press, 1991)

CHRIS ORSMAN (1955–)

ORNAMENTAL GORSE

It's ornamental where it's been
self-sown across the hogback,

obsequious and buttery,
cocking a snook at scars,

yellowing our quaint history
of occupation and reprise.

The spiny tangential crotch,
gullied and decorative,

I love from a distance,
a panorama over water

from lakeside to peninsula
where it's delicate in hollows,

or a topiary under heavens
cropped by the south wind.

I offer this crown of thorns,
for the pity of my countrymen

unconvinced of the beauty
of their reluctant emblem: this

burnt, hacked, blitzed
exotic.

Ornamental Gorse (Victoria University Press, 1994)

THE LAST TENT

Personal to the last, his body
pressed on him a more intimate belief.

What broke down – gristle, fibre,
the scar tissue of old wounds –

was dispensable, bit by bit
succumbing to the grief

he'd all but tutored himself in.
Before the blizzard struck

he saw skuas in clustered flight,
scattering, reforming, far inland

from their native haunts.
He heard the providential cry

from that scant shoreline civilisation,
smelt the wrack of a lightening coast,

the colonies preserved in beloved capes
for which he must soon be bound.

South (Victoria University Press, 1996)

VINCENT O'SULLIVAN (1937–)

The sparrows are taking Seddon
seriously enough to try
making a nest between his feet
that can't – not in this town,
its winds, its preordinations –
last beyond tomorrow noon,
or Friday at latest.

Even the trouser cuffs of the great
can't protect past that.
Yet being sparrows they persist,
they get on with living
between the very feet
of big bronze death,
they work at perdurable shacking

against season,
against weather,
against the choler of experts.
With sparrows, again, perspective
is with means, as ends:
their squabble is with a straw
that almost gets away.

The Rose Ballroom and other Poems (John McIndoe, 1982)

There's a dreary morning coming up,
the sky's as dull as a shoe.
It'll be a day that won't touch
even the last gasp of blue.

The best words won't work –
love and the rest, love
and the glint it's meant to give,
love's as slack as an old glove.

The harbour lies there meek
in a window looking south,
the south and its imagined fangs
in that imagined mouth.

'That'll be the day' as we like
to say, but it won't be today,
'There's a dreary week of it coming up,'
is what we say, and say.

Yet a day when you don't expect it,
sheer glitter ringing about
as if all the cutlery drawers of Kelburn
had been tipped out,

a day when the knives don't nick,
when the dry horizons scale.
There's a shine and flicker to the wind,
southern rancours fail

to cut the ice we expect,
the mountains ride their horses
with their withers of snow,
and the wind, the stroked manes of the horses.

Seeing You Asked (Victoria University Press, 1998)

THE GRIEVING PROCESS

My dad you could say was an illicit substance
in the body politic of family life.

He was flashier, my dad, than spastic traffic
lights, and that was on a quiet day.

The opening night of Milton's big yarn
on an ice-rink laced with lasers

doesn't describe dad either, but it'll do
for the kind of woman who blew his mind.

When I was a child I thought bosom
and Zeppelin must both belong to the Germans,

because mum said God's vengeance
rode high against both, and I knew

from seeing the old man at an office party
that Miss Zelda's Zeppelins must be

an international threat, never mind the Home
Guard. Dad survives on a high-wire

in my mind, spangles and distance
and by Christ, what a fall's coming!

When it came he was like a carpet
you might as well say looked

like dad spread out only thinner than a pikelet.
Oldies' home, tremors, church mice

has numbered accounts if comparisons
mean much. But a bugger and a half

right to the door where the coffin's varnish
crackled. The one bit of his will

he bothered to finish was a woman undertaker
had to lay him out. Must be over forty.

He wasn't responsible if not.
He's a dirty old myth, our dad,

but a source of consolation to me, for one,
who switches off the cricket the moment

I'm instructed, before I make the tea.
He's a big sunset still fading the curtains.

And my sister, who married well,
says does she watch her Eric, thanks to dad.

Seeing You Asked (Victoria University Press, 1998)

HORSES WITH CHILDREN

ALISTAIR PATERSON

Horses with children by a green paddock
       stop the car. In a field of silence
       colder than stars, ears pricking
       the great beasts move gently
       through grass – the children follow
       wind-driven, like ungainly flowers.

We watch while the landscape, strangely
       pale, white as the wood
       of weathered rails, and the sky's
       distant bars bespeak unearthly
       thunder – a struggle of horses
       and men, rain and trampled mud

swept by lightning and coursed
       by flood. Soon the children
       will know that the sky itself
       is the implacable force that throws
       horses and men from a babble
       of fields, the heat of the sun,

that in spite of whatever they say
       or do, there's nothing can ever
       be changed, nothing at all
       to be done. Disturbed by the engine
       the horses start, though faintly
       they sound, the children laugh.

Birds Flying (Pegasus Press, 1973)

PROGRESS

downstairs there are moans
followed by screams . . .

the wall shakes & my bed rattles
as I lie awake & listen.

it's 3 in the morning & these poems
are taking me *nowhere.*

so I get out of bed & glance at
the night sky, thinking that if I had

a needle, I would knit a light refrain
into the woolly clouds

something like, '*Welcome to*
the world, are you having a good time?'

Shoot (Sudden Valley Press, 1999)

VIVIENNE PLUMB (1955–)

BEFORE THE OPERATION

You'll be there in white
you'll drop into the bottom of nowhere
when they give you the needle
I'll hold your hand
while you flake out.

Forefinger and thumb
we're that close,
moi et vous,
(or rather *tu*),
sometimes so hair's breadth
we can't breathe.

The body has a terrestrial
magnetism even when it's unconscious
but the soul
is the one to watch,
possessing wings of its own,
I'll have to weight your's
telling you the wonderful things
about you, yourself, and your life.

Salamanca (HeadworX, 1998)

TAPEWORM

The journey is now within me,
a tapeworm
invading my gut,
the larvae have hatched.

At night my feet
make walking motions
ball to toe
muffled between the sheets,
in my sleep I am free
to promenade my own dreams.

I am getting to know them.
Me and my dreams
shake hands,
at first we made small chat
but now we are intimate
with one another every night,
and each position is exceptional.

Avalanche (Pemmican Press, 2000)

ROMA POTIKI (1958–)

P

HERS IS

The moon does not have
a strategic plan

She is not owned by a corporate
her pull is not a hand
or a bank balance,
Dow Jones means nothing to her.

Hers is
a going towards
and a return,
a hiss and a roar
a spit and polish
a shaving of paua backs
to produce a showing.

She can dance
she can
can wave her hips and laugh
knowingly,
what a woman
moves as she
must.

Yes
I knew her
a small beacon in the world.

To me she was a bonfire
a torch setting itself alight
on a beach
in a limited season.

Shaking the Tree (Steele Roberts, 1998)

You have such
clever hands.

You hold the islands
on the tips of your
fingers, lightly so

you never submerge
them. Firmly enough that
they don't float away.

If a person could hold
another person like that –
well, then

there would only be
love.

Auckland University Press New Poets 1 (Auckland University Press,
1999)

LAURA RANGER (1985–)

THE SEA

the mist smudges out
Kapiti Island

the hills curve and rise
like loaves of bread

the sun sprinkles glitter
on the sea

the wind is writing
what it knows
in lines along the water

Laura's Poems (Godwit, 1995)

DONA NOBIS PACEM

for Pamela

You had no wish to leave this world and time
or us, but knew that in the way of things you would.
Without the indulgence of fancy, allow us to let you
go with the innumerable angels.

Not everyone can hear the things they need to
most, or tell them. I never had the chance
to tell you what I'd learned of Robert Carver –
voices in the vault of God, lifting, turning as a
film will take your eyes round corners
unsuspected, into naves and arches, liberated texts
of stone, cavernous cathedral space, pillars of sound supporting
the weight, rivers of voice, carrying rafts of us onward, on
parabolas of song: registers of penitence,
humility, and faith.

This morning at eight I heard you had died in the night,
at four. The lowest segment of the clock
closed in; night filled it, carried
the news to me, waking to the winter dawn.

At ten I played the six-part mass
and listened to it for you,
soaring, ascending, leaving us
things that are living
always so easily hurt.

> *Agnus Dei,*
qui tollis peccata mundi:
miserere nobis; dona nobis pacem.

First & Last Songs (Auckland University Press, 1995)

HARRY RICKETTS (1950–)

Lie jet-lagged in Rome in the half-dark.
(Listen to the bells.)
The kids are still fast asleep
unlike the young Americans next door
going pell-mell all night.

Light is already beginning
to lick through the shutters.
(Listen to the bells.)
Was it for this you flew back
across the world? Well, was it?

You're thirty-five; that's the age
for reverting to type or at least
for telling the story so far.
(Listen to the bells.)
They say the truth is

you'll never be other
than the self you are. But it's
all right. The light is
shining bars across the room.
Just listen to the bells.

Coming Here (Nagare Press, 1989)

THE MOMENT

Selection of the moment
should be undertaken with care.
Bear in mind that you will have
total recall in the years to come.

Avoid thunderstorms. Gothic
effects may be spectacular
but the last thing you want is
to end up frozen, alone and wet.

Not in front of the children;
it's cruel and bound to fail.
Don't forget that even great
tragedy neighbours soap opera.

An exotic location
is best. The picturesque backdrop
will neatly complement what
may grow more poignant in memory.

Be sure to write your own script;
then at least you'll know what you said.
Under no circumstances use
the final scene from *Casablanca.*

How Things Are (Whitireia Publishing and Daphne Brasell Ass.,
1996)

THE TEST

Of the seven stars
in the Pleiades
I can still make out four
on a moonless night,
if I don't look too hard,
slightly to one side.

Of the possibly sixteen
lines to this poem,
in doubts and uncertainties
I make out seven;
and the shape of the last is
growing clearer . . .

For Blackfoot warriors
the test of keen sight
was to number the Pleiades.

Now I too
must account for them all.

Poetry New Zealand II (Pegasus Press, 1974)

RIVERSDALE

There are towns in the South
you wouldn't dip your head-
lights for: the hotel
the store, the service station

and they're gone, a quick
hiatus on the plain.
Whatever your thirst
it must stay unquenched;

for even the Mobil man
is not so obliging
he'll stand to attention
all night. And whatever lights

still let on that anyone's
at home, gaze inwards
incommunicado.
                The dark
and the distance must

still be kept out
and above all you Northerners
who talk as fast
as you drive; who rap

on the counter expecting
instant service. Who think
that the South can be subdued
in a single transit.

El Sur (Pemmican Press, 1998)

ON IMPULSE

So you decided to get up that morning,
to have (for example) muesli for breakfast
instead of porridge (because it was almost
summer), to take the car instead of the bus,
and to switch lanes without first checking. So
you got away with it that time, and you
don't normally take risks, but you'd figured
that the woman you'd married would prove
more enduring than the one with the laugh;
that a stumble on the front step wouldn't
alter the course of history; that the exploded
hedgehog on the road wouldn't be a setback
to evolution, or a premonition; that a mid-week
flit over the Antarctic would beat going to work
(as indeed it did). So you left the house
in a hurry, forgetting your binoculars,
your false teeth, and the time, and you took
your position amongst the casualties,
strapped yourself in, picked up your pen
and drafted that report that was a little too
intemperate for its own good, typed the number
six instead of four into the programme,
and altered another kind of course (yours),
so assembling an unsuspecting cast who were
at that moment eating muesli instead
of porridge (or not), and who were also taking
steps that would have ramifications that
would never stop branching in their scraggly
fashion. So you set out that morning, and so
you let that aircraft, its pilots, and so many
decisions carry you to the South, out of your
own hands, out of reach, and out of time.
So you decided; and so you died.

Erebus. A poem (Hazard Press, 1999)

SMOKE

Like every Glasgwegian
in the 1920s
my father was born with smouldering lips.
Unless a cigarette was inserted
his mouth tasted wrong to him.

Oil from the lathes he worked
year in, year out damaged his skin
but he hated to wear gloves,
wanting nothing more on his hands but
a lit fag and his wedding ring.

While still waist-high to him, I tried
once to calculate his consumption –
forty a day, multiplied by
the days in a year, times
the years in my father's life.

It was too hard for me. I recall
how in my father's final week
he unearthed a packet of long-
mislaid filter-tips and, grinning, said
perhaps this was an omen, perhaps

his luck soon would change. The evening
of his cremation I tried not to look
where the vapours that were my father
rose to join factory fumes and the ghosts
of his seven million cigarettes.

S

KEITH SINCLAIR (1922–1993)

The bomb is made will drop on Rangitoto.
Be kind to one another, kiss a little
And let love-making imperceptibly
Grow inwards from a kiss. I've done with soldiering,
Though every day my leave-pass may expire.

The bomb is made will drop on Rangitoto.
The cell of death is formed that multiplied
Will occupy the lung, exclude the air.
Be kind to one another, kiss a little –
The first goodbye might each day last forever.

The bomb is made will drop on Rangitoto.
The hand is born that gropes to press the button.
The prodigal grey generals conspire
To dissipate the birthright of the Asians.
Be kind to one another, kiss a little.

The bomb is made will drop on Rangitoto.
The plane that takes off persons in a hurry
Is only metaphorically leaving town,
So if we linger we will be on time.
Be kind to one another, kiss a little.

The bomb is made will drop on Rangitoto.
I do not want to see that sun-burned harbour,
Islandless as moon, red-skied again,
Its tide unblossomed, sifting wastes of ash.
Be kind to one another, kiss a little,
Our only weapon is this gentleness.

Moontalk (Auckland University Press, 1993)

HERE COME THE CLOUDS

Here come the clouds the same as last June
Puffy like the breasts of birds, one . . . two . . . three . . .
They have circumnavigated the world
Birds heavy from flight, home again.

A year has passed. Now they fill the sky
Thicker and thicker having no other place to go.
What is the end of navigation then? They seem
Swollen as though their arteries of air

Ached from memory as well and
Dilated their hearts so they come
Weighed with longing for their homeland.
And here they are. Is this it then?
This empty sky, waiting.

The Tudor Style: Poems New and Selected (Auckland University
Press, 1993)

CITY GIRL IN THE COUNTRY

The rooster crows like someone being sick.
How Nature stinks! The fecund pots
Of time-embalming herbs visibly
Eat what sun there is embalming us.
The proper oils, the proper bread
Seem offerings to a beetling god
Whose hair sprouts under the flagstones
Whose orisons arise in fleas.
The busy ant, pernicious wasp
Devour their mutual hemispheres.
The girl in the garden calls out 'Shit!'
Aimlessly pulling out the weeds.

You're Very Seductive William Carlos Williams (John McIndoe, 1978)

MY MOTHER LOOKING AT STARS

Each morning in the small hours
my mother pads from bed and back
with a pause for stargazing.

Her body wakes her. The stars watch her.
What connects them: this she puzzles
and finds pleasure in no answer

but three elements: flesh, spirit
and steely starlight. I count
she thinks, because I am aware

and care to look at stars for a moment
allowing them to wake me, more than
my body does, being a craft

merely. While their gaze judges
with benignity the watcher of the watchers.
I am close to stars in the night.

The Lark Quartet (Auckland University Press, 1999)

KENDRICK SMITHYMAN (1922–1995)

Walk past those houses on a Sunday morning
where pianos stumble in front rooms,
mechanics freed from tools take shears
to clip their hedges, talking politics.

Or move along the lake, or down a track
prop against butts of logs and eye the mangroves,
flip pottery shards and chips as distant farms
grow up from fog to sun. Remember, it was here
pedantic summer rose to read the lesson.

Think, how threads were drawing close together:
detail a month, day, hour and an ungainly
kitbag lugged home in the tram, two days later
put down in the hot Waikato close to the river –
bell tents, new straw, uniforms everywhere.

Leave was a chance to take your bike
crawling into the ranges, were places
not to be seen as before, and places to visit:
a house with oaks where one was quick
with sympathy, but did not understand.

Count them again, these things, the League ball
punted across the park, processional
sails of eighteen footers, cold salad at five.

Somewhere there's value to them. As a piano stumbles
something comes into being. It will take shape in the end.

Selected Poems (Auckland University Press, 1989)

Somewhere, away inland, that we decay is
Less pleasantly recalled to us. Mortality
Arranges signs and wistfully flies
The sad gulls from us, where human pity
Or manly ambition are mainly irrelevant,
Fronted by surflines or warmly pondered
Arrested among dunes of spinifex.

Although you truly argue in this mood
The facts, of course, are frankly otherwise.
It is ambition which now regulates these dunes
Planning a future for them as a forest.
Pity perhaps is what presumes our taste,
Hearing of graves found by oven stones, an ear
Pendant recovered from solitary bones.

How one recurs, to graves and talk of bones.
Decay is the first most primitive order
Given this beach by its curious hidden creatures
To whom, loaded with diatoms, tides come
Seeding thirty close miles of sand with shells,
Living and dead sustained in one regimen:
Feed, propagate, be fed on; please someone; die.

Selected Poems (Auckland University Press, 1989)

CHARLES SPEAR (1910–1985)

That was the prelude. Silver snow
Like spangles sifted through the rhododendron leaves,
Chimed on the spider-webs, swept to and fro,
And blurred the lawn, the urns, the drooping eaves.

So after bitter exile he came home
And found it smashed, by Prussian gunfire overset.
One guest remained, an abbé or a gnome,
Who, cross-legged, rolled a cigarette
And shared with scampering mice a sugared violet.

Twopence Coloured (Caxton Press, 1951)

CAMERA

The camera tongue quick
licks at the moment,
sticks into place
the instant forever.

Time feels no trace
of the image skimmed,
flicked from its skin,
does not know it has been
minutely tricked.

Landfall 125 (March 1978)

MARY STANLEY (1919–1980)

HOUSEHOLDER

Never build a house to the south, they say.
It's cold. The sun goes north on holiday,
the nights are bitter, even the fleas retreat.

But summer, ah, summer is another time.
The flimsy house is hot enough, the doors
and windows gape to catch a breath of air.

And yet I like this house under the pines.
We have mended the roof, painted the walls, set all
in order. Only the garden will not be tamed.

No manual can coax this stubborn earth
to bloom. Sometimes we blame the pines, and laugh
knowing our lazy ways. The weeds rejoice.

The Starveling Year and Other Poems (Auckland University Press,
1994)

Being a woman, I am
not more than man nor less
but answer imperatives
of shape and growth. The bone
attests the girl with dolls,
grown up to know the moon
unwind her tides to chafe
the heart. A house designs
my day an artifact
of care to set the hands
of clocks, and hours are round
with asking eyes. Night puts
an ear on silence where
a child may cry. I close
my books and know events
are people, and all roads
everywhere walk home
women and men, to take
history under their roofs.
I see Icarus fall
out of the sky, beside
my door, not beautiful,
envy of angels, but feathered
for a bloody death.

The Starveling Year and Other Poems (Auckland University Press, 1994)

C.K. STEAD (1932–)

I was caned often at school.
Only once so it mattered.
His name was Tammy Scott.
I never knew him use a cane
Except just once – on me.
He taught maths,
Promoted a small pianist
Who grew to be a big one,
And painted bowls of roses
In a fine dead style.
He used the names and dates
Of the school's two hundred war-dead
To make a book,
One fine laborious painted page
For each dead old-boy.

I used a pen-knife,
Hacked my impertinent name
On the top of a desk. STEAD.
Was it the bald style
Of a life-inscription
That so distressed him?

Nothing had prepared me
In that empty cloakroom
For Tammy's violence.
He went. When he came back
I was still where I'd stopped
My forehead sweating
Against the panelled wall.

I think of Tammy
Who meant no harm
Labouring among the dead.

I walked past him, and out.
I looked at him, not 'daggers',
But truly without feeling.
He might have been a desk-top.
My pride was exact.
I would not go down
In Tammy's book.
He would go down in mine.

Crossing the Bar (Auckland University Press/Oxford University
Press, 1972)

from **QUESADA**

'*Je pense . . .*

aux vaincus!'

1

All over the plain of the world lovers are being hurt.
The spring wind takes up their cries and scatters them to the clouds.
Juan Quesada hears them. By the world at large they go unheard.
Only those in pain can hear the chorus of pain.
High in the air over winds that shake the leaves
High over traffic, beyond bird call, out of the reach of silence
These lovers are crying out because the spring has hurt them.
No one dies of that pain, some swear by it, a few will live with it always,
No one mistakes it for the lamentations of hell
Because there is a kind of exaltation in it
More eloquent than the tongues of wind and water
More truthful than the sibylline language of the leaves
The cry of the injured whose wounds are dear to them
The howl of the vanquished who cherish their defeat.

Quesada (The Shed, 1975)

3

October, and the kowhais declare themselves through parks
And gardens, and along the bush road to Karekare

As if someone had called on the faithful each to light a candle
And through a darkened arena the yellow flames

In their thousands flared into life. I know the darkness
These flowers make known, a spirit like water gathered

In a cup of nasturtium leaves at morning – black water
That lines the cup with silver. Let's say it's because

One evening thirty years ago as I walked to scouts
The world unveiled itself and through me burned

An ecstasy of which each moment after of life
Harbours an echo – as these kowhais hide themselves

Till the season calls them forth. My books advise
I will know that ecstasy once more before I die.

Walking Westward (The Shed, 1979)

J.C. STURM (1927–)

The bones of my tupuna
Safe in secret places up north
Must wait a little longer
Before they claim me for good.

        The love of my second parents
        Unconditional from the beginning
        Unrelenting to the end
        Never quite made me theirs.

That tormented paradoxical man
Father of my children
Convinced me we belonged together
But then moved on.

        The young ones (our young) he left behind
        Claimed my castle as their own
        Being themselves a part of me
        Always, bone of my bone.

Years earlier, a much younger self
Lay face down in hot dry sand –

        Salt on her skin, the smell
        Of green flax pungent in the heat,
        Summer a korowai
        Around bare shoulders –

And felt in her bones
Without knowing why
She belonged to that place.

Nearly a life-time later

On another beach –

                            the sea
        A blinking shield at our feet,
        Behind us a dark hill fortress
        With sentinel sea birds
        Circling and calling –
I lay down beside you in tussock
And felt without warning
I had come home.

Dedications (Steele Roberts, 1996)

S

ROBERT SULLIVAN (1967–)

If waka could be resurrected
they wouldn't just come out
from museum doors smashing
glass cases revolving and sliding
doors on their exit.

they wouldn't just come out
of mountains as if liquidified
from a frozen state
the resurrection wouldn't just
come about this way

the South Island turned to wood
waiting for the giant crew
of Maui and his brothers
bailers and anchors turned back
to what they were when they were strewn

about the country by Kupe
and his relations
the resurrection would happen
in the blood of the men and women
the boys and girls

who are blood relations
of the crews whose veins
touch the veins who touched the veins
of those who touched the veins
who touched the veins

who touched the veins
of the men and women from the time
of Kupe and before.
The resurrection will come
out of their blood.

Star Waka (Auckland University Press, 1999)

Once hangi grew
like melon pregnant bellies
full of black and white flesh.

Now the stones are cold.
Te Kooti is dead
under incubus earth.

We are ashes of his fire
dead a hundred years.

Safe in our houses
we have stripped him
to a feather in the wind
as distant as a morepork
that calls in the night.

Eyes of the Ruru (Voice Press, 1979)

LIKE LAMPLIGHT

BRIAN TURNER (1944–)

One day when you are beside me
invite me to speak
of the secrets I never knew
I wanted to tell you, of the warmth
I never knew I owned
until you released it
by moving close as lamplight seems
to glass. Ask me

why I came to you
with the reverence of one
who sees a flower bloom
where none has bloomed before.
By saying what is
I will have said what was.

Sometimes when you are content
ask me what it is
that moves me to want to hold you so,
so often, and laugh when I tell
you the same old
indestructible thing.

One day when you are
where you need no invitation to be
I will tell you
how you flower
like lamplight in me.

Ancestors (John McIndoe, 1981)

MADRIGAL

The moon rose out of the sea
    and climbed above Mihiwaka.
        How terrible, lonely and far off
            it seemed, how resolute and cold

in a vast nest of stars.
    I stood leaning on a gatepost
        listening to the mysterious wind
            bending the pines a long time

before I set off back down the hill
    felling like a stranger
        returning to the place
            where he was born.

And the moon came after me,
    sat on my shoulder
        and followed me inside.
            All night it lay glowing

in the bones of my body,
    a private pain, given over
        to everything; all night
            the moon glowed as a body glows

in a halo of moonlight,
    and in the half-light of dawn
        I heard the moon sing a madrigal
            for those who live alone.

Ancestors (John McIndoe, 1981)

FINGERBONES

You'd be amazed,
noting our brittleness,
how we used
to lovingly clench
and cup. Flesh
formed the shape
but we provided
the framework.
When the heart
leapt we moved
like hit men,
quickly, efficiently.
Cold, limp, clammy,
we were expert
at putting people
off, when we
wanted to.
      Yet what joy
we knew, and what
trauma, what shame.

When we were young
we were steady
and we never
shook with passion
or desperation.
We fluttered
like moths
in moonlight.
Later we fumbled,
fondled, stroked,
caressed. We
beckoned, dismissed.
We've been into

everything at one
time or another.

Once, when we broke
down, flesh and sinew
had to wait
until we mended.
It was nice
to hold the upper
hand.
            But that's past.
Now we lie here
praising the virtues
of interdependence
and when we're stood on
we go click and snap
just like we used
to do when we craved
undivided attention.

Bones (John McIndoe, 1985)

HONE TUWHARE (1922–)

Where are the men of mettle?
    are there old scores
    left to settle?
    when will the canoes leap
    to the stab and kick
    the sea-wet flourish
    of pointed paddles?
    will the sun play again
    to the skip of muscles
    on curved backs bared
    to the rain's lash
    the sea's punch?
    to War! to War!

where are the proud lands
    to subdue – and women?
    where are the slaves
    to gather wood for the fires
    stones for the oven?
    who shall reap
    the succulent children whimpering
    on the terraced hill-top?

no more alas no more
    no raw memory left
    of these
    nor bloody trophies:
    only the fantail's flip
    to cheeky war-like postures
    and on the sand-hill
    wry wind fluting
    the bleached bones marrowless

Mihi: Collected Poems (Penguin, 1987)

HEEMI

for James K. Baxter

No point now my friend in telling
you my lady's name.
She wished us well: ordered wheels
which spun my son and me like
comets through the lonely night.
You would have called her Aroha.

And when we picked up three young
people who'd hitched their way
from the Ninety Mile Beach to be
with you, I thought: yes
your mana holds, Heemi. Your mana
is love. And suddenly the night
didn't seem lonely anymore.

The car never played up at all.
And after we'd given it a second
gargle at the all-night bowser
it just zoomed on on gulping
easily into the gear changes
up or down.

Because you've been over this road
many times before Heemi, you'd
know about the steady climb ahead
of us still. But once in the tricky
light, Tongariro lumbered briefly
out of the clouds to give us the old
'up you' sign. Which was real friendly.

When we levelled off a bit at the top
of the plateau, the engine heat couldn't
keep the cold from coming in: the fog
swamping thick and slushy, and pressing
whitely against tired eyeballs.

Finally, when we'd eased ourselves
over a couple of humps and down down
the winding metalled road to the river
and Jerusalem, I knew things would be
all right. Glad that others from the
Mainland were arrowing toward the dawn
like us.

Joy for the brother sun chesting over
the brim of the land, and for the three
young blokes flaked out in the back seat
who would make it now, knowing that they
were not called on to witness
some mysterious phenomenon of birth on
a dung-littered floor of a stable

but come simply to call
on a tired old mate in a tent
laid out in a box
with no money in the pocket
no fancy halo, no thump left in the old
ticker.

Mihi: Collected Poems (Penguin, 1987)

It didn't make a grand entrance and I nearly
missed it – tip-toeing up on me as it did
when I was half asleep and suddenly, they're there
before my eyes – white pointillist flakes
on a Hotere canvas – swirling about on untethered

gusts of air and spreading thin uneven
thicknesses of white snow-cover on drooping
ti-kouka leaves, rata, a lonely kauri, pear
and beech tree. Came without hesitation
right inside my opened window licking my neck

my arms my nose as I leaned far out to embrace
a phantom sky above the house-tops
and over the sea: '*Hey, where's the horizon?*
I shall require a boat you know – two strong arms?'
. . . and snow, kissing and lipping my face

gently, mushily, like a pet whale,
or (if you prefer) a shark with red bite – sleet
sting hot as ice. Well,
it's stopped now. Stunning sight. Unnerved,
the birds have stopped singing,

tucking their beaks under warm armpits: temporarily.
And for miles upon whitened miles around,
there is no immediate or discernible movement,
except from me, transfixed, and moved by an interior
agitation – an armless man applauding.

'Bravo,' I whisper. 'Bravissimo.' Standing ovation.
Why not . . . Oh, come in, Spring.

Mihi: Collected Poems (Penguin, 1987)

RAE VARCOE (1944–)

you are scheduled for Thursday for your operation
on Wednesday [2–3 p.m.] report to reception
a deposit of $200 for each admission day is required
credit cards suffice here, but cash or cheque is nicer

on Wednesday [2–3 p.m.] report to reception
please bring toiletries, nightwear and dressing gown
credit cards suffice here, but cash or cheque is nicer
before leaving you must settle your debit entirely

please bring toiletries, nightwear and dressing gown
you may be unable to walk at discharge
before leaving you must settle your debit entirely
and later claim for insurance (if any)

you may be unable to walk at discharge
wheelchairs and crutches are an added charge
later claim for insurance (if any)
cash or cheque are preferred, yours faithfully, . . .

wheelchairs and crutches are an added charge
remember, payment may not be deferred
cash or cheque are preferred, yours faithfully, . . .
'*God's mercy endures for ever*'

remember, payment may not be deferred
a deposit of $200 for each admission day is required
'*God's mercy endures for ever*'
you are scheduled for Thursday for your operation

New Zealand Books 30 (October 1997)

WATCHING SNOW

You were standing at the window, silently
when the first flakes began to fall
between the houses, to settle on the boughs
of the leafless elm and in the yard below;
and so intently were you watching them
spin through the early winter gloom
to catch in fences, heap the window sill,
you did not notice when I spoke to you.

So I fell silent, too, But no,
not just because the snow enchanted me:
the way you stood there like a memory
re-awakened so much tenderness
I had thought buried long ago,
nostalgic, maternal as the falling snow,
that I was glad when you made no reply.
Nearness enough to watch you standing there,

and as intently as you watched the snow:
it gathered slowly, darkening your hair
and shoulders, till your outline only, drained
like a negative, at last remained,
sharp against the window veiled with steam.
You must have known that I was watching you,
pierced by the memory a snowflake clears,
or why you were also, when you turned, in tears.

Settler and Stranger (Caxton Press, 1965)

IAN WEDDE (1946–)

50

for Robin & Lois

Cast off   earth-ferry! forever into
your own presence
                    under the shining sails
of your firmament
                    among galaxies
archipelagos the colour of stars
endless oceans continents star-harbours . . .

au revoir
    so long
                    bon voyage Charlie
have a wonderful time. Planets also
are lofted by those convections   they are
kites carried by your breath Carlos   the sail
sings in the updraughts of your blood   forever!

into *this* presence
                    where you are sleeping
& dreaming under Robin's plum tree, small
& mysterious as well, a traveller
like the rest of us
                    dreaming of travelling.

Earthly: Sonnets for Carlos (Amphedesma Press, 1975)

THE WINDY BOUGH

for Leone

Dear Lee happy birthday now you are older
but not much wiser
I hope: pay no attention to the people
who tell you not to hang your life savings

on that windy bough: it's nearly spring
our lives are ruled by giant corporations
I admit with shame I cheered when I heard
that Nelson Rockefeller's son had disappeared in New Guinea

the *Readers' Digest* & Dale Carnegie
and probably *National Geographic*
certainly *Time* magazine
                              are trying to
turn our brains into stir-n-serve

mush. Mush! 'Nanook of the North'
is a very sexy film starring Anouk Aimé
as an eskimo maid smeared with walrus fat
'Yellow Snow' is a song by Frank Zappa

about husky pee
                              but free association gets you nowhere
in the end and who needs them? (Ends.
Life as a series of unclosed parentheses
is what gives me hope and confidence: knowing

all those right-hand hugs await me
at the terminus))))))))))))))))))))))
your shock waves travelling on into Eternity
which is a nice thought for your birthday dear Lee

the beautiful world is such a mess
the most important thing you can do is be as kind to your
friends as you are stake everything on your windy bough
sit up on it & sing your great big heart out

Georgicon (Victoria University Press, 1984)

SIX FALSE STARTS. NO STOPS. GETTING HOMESICK.

Somewhere behind all this, before a view
of fountains, statues and grass,
near a lake, far from you.

Somewhere behind all this,
stranded in language neither advancing
nor falling back.

Between desire and absence, in a mill of meaning,
grinding between language and the
words I want to speak.

Moving towards you somewhere behind all this,
moving back from this, moving
behind this, to where the language of desire

and the words I have for you
are ground
between desire and absence.

Hesitant, provisional, urgent, moving myself
into that grinding place,
feeling myself grounded

somewhere behind all this,
becoming the words which
have entered the place of you.

Becoming absent in the place of you,
the space you name, the space of your name,
moving behind all this, the fountains,

the statues and grass, the lake. Ground
to be whispered by you, your
desire, my absence. That place.

The Drummer (Auckland University Press, 1993)

PARENTS & CHILDREN

Parents and their children come
to one another through many doors
that laugh, slap, clap, slash, bleed
block, cry, and let-you-through sometimes.
And by the time they meet
they've been sieved to the rags and bones
of who they were and can't remember.

Around our house mynah birds
dart and dive. I count
the holes they pierce in the sky.
My son is in the garage fixing
the brakes of his bike.
In her bedroom my daughter
is locked into Captain America.

I've left believing in God,
my children are starting towards Him.
I carry willingly the heritage of my Dead,
my children have yet to recognize theirs.
Someday before they leave our house
forever I'll tell them: 'Our Dead
are the splendid robes our souls wear.'

The armada of mynah birds continues
to attack the trees and sky.
Their ferocity cuts wounds
in my thoughts.
Through those wounds like doors
I'll go this morning
to meet my children.

Shaman of Visions (Auckland University Press/Oxford University Press,
1984)

VIRGINIA WERE (1960–)

W

COMING DOWN, WEST AUCKLAND, 7.10.98

You are the blue neon ladder I climb
into the high, arcing dusk.
At this time of day, as shreds
of cloud ignite above the Waitakeres,
my spirit escapes its prison
– leaping hillsides,

seeping into darkened valleys,
along high-tension lines,
the gridded pylons that carry light
the length of the North Island.

It's only when I drive down from the hills
into wine-growing country and orchards,
past the long grey shadow of the poultry
shed on Old North Road, that my feet
touch the ground – the worn, squeaking
pedals of accelerator and brake.

I stop at the intersection where there
are always several cars for sale
and it's just another dusk.
The red neon sign above the takeaway
on Brigham Creek Road seeps into
the ordinary, grainy dark.

Jump Start (Victoria University Press, 1999)

TODAY'S STORY

There it is again,
a plaintive call in the cypress,
four notes endlessly repeated

in the threadbare hall of winter:
witness, witness, witness, witness
the long decline of the sun

into clouds, driven
by the glimmer of the bird singing
its chorus of days without

love. And why,
in the weak soup of the day,
does the bird seem to follow,

incessantly there?
It laments for those who are
falling, swept

in the floodtide of their lives,
wishing to be more than the husked
skin of their longing. The song

is unanswerable, unmelodic. There are
no clothes in which to dress the nakedness
of fear. We fear less

when the world is naked with us.
The small bird, a thumb print only,
sings and sings, notes like dust all over the trees.

The Ambiguous Companion (Hazard Press, 1996)

PATRICK WILSON (1926–1999)

The oyster shuts his gates to form the pearl.
He knows he has a saviour caught within him,
Poor fool, old oyster. And it works against him,
An irritant that's locked within his shell,
A single-mindedness that thins his heart,
Turns it to narrowheartedness. Yet he,
Poor fool, poor oyster, used to love the sea
In all its many forms, to every part
Open with tranquil, unassuming jaws.
Then that foul irritant was driven in,
And snap! the wounded tongue cherished its sin
Until at last by hard, immobile laws
    A shining, perfect pebble made from wrong –
    A perfect grievance – rolled from off the tongue.

The Bright Sea (Pegasus Press, 1950)

THE SMILE

For a pound I buy an old Ink Spots LP.
The girl behind the desk gives me a sort of
sincere, kind smile, and I am grateful.
I'd not expected it, only my change.

Into the Golden Lion now for lunch,
and here, although all that I'm looking for
is a ham sandwich, a glass of wine, again
the gent behind the bar gives me that smile,

that lovely smile, the smile the young ones keep
for non-combatants, the deferential old.

At the Window & Other Poems (Nag's Head Press, 1997)

KING OF KINGS

HUBERT WITHEFORD (1921–2000)

The Emperor (you've heard?) went by this road.
Ahead, police, postillions, cuirassiers;
Behind, ambassadors, air-marshals, equerries,
And, all around, this mild, unjubilant crowd.
I saw the Emperor?
Well, no. It seemed important to be there.
I'd travelled far. Spent my life's savings, too.
But, while I looked at the half-witted horsemen's plumes
And thought of some of what was wrong with me,
I saw his back, receding down new streets.

A Native, Perhaps Beautiful (Caxton Press, 1967)

GOING INTO WINTER

I am in the full blast.
Never
I begin to understand
Was I ever
Out of it.

Usually
The trees relax gradually
Into nakedness
But today the leaves hurtle past me.

Each morning
I wake earlier
Mourning
The chances
That will never happen again,

Welcoming
The deluded sparrows
Who think it is dawn.

A Blue Monkey for the Tomb (Faber, 1994)

DAVID McKEE WRIGHT (1869–1928)

The moon is bright, and the winds are laid, and the river is
    roaring by;
Orion swings, with his belted lights low down in the western
    sky;
North and south from the mountain gorge to the heart of the
    silver plain
There's many an eye will see no sleep till the east grows
    bright again;
There's many a hand will toil to-night, from the centre down
    to the sea;
And I'm far from the men I used to know – and my love is far
    from me.

Where the broad flood eddies the dredge is moored to the
    beach of shingle white,
And the straining cable whips the stream in a spray of silver
    light;
The groaning buckets bear their load, and the engine throbs
    away,
And the wash pours red on the turning screen that knows not
    night or day;
For there's many an ounce of gold to save, from the gorge to
    the shining sea –
And there's many a league of the bare brown hills between
    my love and me.

Where the lines of gorse are parched and dry, and the sheaves
    are small and thin,
The engine beats and the combine sings to the drays that are
    leading in,
For they're thrashing out of the stook to-night, and the plain
    is as bright as day,
And the fork-tines flash as the sheaves are turned on the frame
    of the one-horse dray;
For many a hand will toil to-night, from the mountains down
    to the sea; –

But I'm far from the lips of the girl I love, and the heart that
    beats for me.

The trappers are out on the hills to-night, and the sickly
    lantern-shine
Is mocking the gleam of the silver moon in the scrub on the
    long trap-line;
The tallies are big on the rock-strewn spur, and the rattling
    clink of the chain
Comes weirdly mixed from the moon-bright hill with the
    whistling shriek of pain;
For many a hand will toil to-night where the tussocks are
    waving free; –
But it's over the hills and over the plain to the heart that
    beats for me.

The stars are bright, and the night is still, and the river is
    singing by,
And many a face is upward turned to gaze at the moon's
    bright eye.
North and south, from the forest deeps to the heart of the
    silver plain,
There's many an eye will see no sleep till the east grows
    bright again;
There's many a hand will toil to-night by the shining land and sea.
O moonlight, bear my message of love to the heart that beats
    for me.

The Station Ballads & Other Verses (John A. Lee, 1945)

ACKNOWLEDGEMENTS

The publishers gratefully acknowledge the following authors, publishers, literary agencies and copyright holders for permission to reproduce the following poems. AUP = Auckland University Press, VUP = Victoria University Press, OUP = Oxford University Press.

'For Andrew', 'Parting is Such Sweet Sorrow', 'Cattle in Mist', © Fleur Adcock and/or OUP

'Springtime', © John Allison and/or Sudden Valley Press

'Im Abendrot' (*from* The Four Last Songs of Richard Strauss at Takahe Creek above the Kaipara), 'The Tall Wind', © Ken Arvidson

'High Country Weather', 'The Ballad of Calvary Street', 'Tomcat', 'Jerusalem Sonnets', © the estate of James K. Baxter and/or OUP

'The Cicadas', © the estate of James Bertram

'Garden-Lion', 'Fall', 'October, 1935', © the estate of Ursula Bethell and/or VUP

'Dancing Bear', 'The Male Voice', © Tony Beyer and/or Melaleuca Press/ Dead Poets Books

'Countries Lodge in the Body', © Paola Bilbrough and/or VUP

'Wellington' (*from* My Side of the Story), 'Mr Maui at Buckingham Palace', © Peter Bland

'Instructions for How to Get Ahead of Yourself While the Light Still Shines', 'The Visit', © Jenny Bornholdt and/or VUP

'Nineteen Thirty-nine', 'Break and Go', 'Winter Anemones', © the estate of Charles Brasch and/or OUP

'Blatant Resistance', 'Wild Daisies', © Bub Bridger and/or Mallinson Rendel

'Tremors', © James Brown and/or VUP

'Look Here', © Rachel Bush and/or VUP

'Broken Glass to Evening Dress', © Kate Camp and/or VUP

BIBLIOGRAPHY

Adcock, Fleur, *Looking Back*, Oxford University Press, London, 1997.
— *The Eye of the Hurricane*, A.H. & A.W. Reed, Wellington/Auckland, 1964.
— *Tigers*, Oxford University Press, London, 1967.

Allison, John, *Stone Moon Dark Water*, Sudden Valley Press, Christchurch, 1999.

Arvidson, Ken, *Riding the Pendulum*, Oxford University Press, Wellington, 1973.

Baughan, B.E., *Reuben and Other Poems*, Constable, London, 1903.

Baxter, James K., *Collected Poems* (ed John Weir), Oxford University Press, Wellington, 1979.

Bertram, James, *Occasional Verses*, Wai-te-ata Press, Wellington, 1971.

Bethell, Ursula, *Collected Poems* (ed Vincent O'Sullivan), Victoria University Press, Wellington, 1997.

Beyer, Tony, *Dancing Bear*, Melaleuca Press, Canberra, 1981.
— *The Male Voice*, Dead Poets Books, Auckland, 1998.

Bilbrough, Paola, *bell tongue*, Victoria University Press, Wellington, 1999.

Bland, Peter, *Mr Maui*, London Magazine Editions, London, 1976.
— *My Side of the Story*, Mate Books, Auckland, 1964.

Bornholdt, Jenny, *Moving House*, Victoria University Press, Wellington, 1989.
— *Waiting Shelter*, Victoria University Press, Wellington, 1991.

Brasch, Charles, *Collected Poems* (ed Alan Roddick), Oxford University Press, 1984.

Bridger, Bub, *Up Here on the Hill*, Mallinson Rendel, Wellington, 1989.

Brown, James, *Go Round Power Please*, Victoria University Press, Wellington, 1996.

Bush, Rachel, *The Hungry Woman*, Victoria University Press, Wellington, 1997.

Camp, Kate, *Unfamiliar Legends of the Stars*, Victoria University Press, Wellington, 1998.

Campbell, Alistair Te Ariki, *Pocket Collected Poems*, Hazard Press, Christchurch, 1996.

Campbell, Meg, *A Durable Fire,* Te Kotare Press, Wellington, 1982.

Cape, Peter, *Peter Cape's Kiwi Ballads*, Kiwi Pacific Records, 1960.

Cochrane, Geoff, *Aztec Noon*, Victoria University Press, Wellington, 1992.

Curnow, Allen, *Early Days Yet, Poems 1941–1997*, Auckland University Press, Auckland, 1997.

Dallas, Ruth, *Day Book*, Caxton Press, Christchurch, 1966.
— *Steps of the Sun*, Caxton Press, Christchurch, 1979.
— *Walking on the Snow*, Caxton Press, Christchurch, 1976.

Dickson, John, *What happened on the way to Oamaru*, Untold Press, Christchurch, 1986.

Dowling, Basil, *Windfalls & Other Poems*, The Nag's Head Press, Christchurch, 1983.

Duggan, Eileen, *Selected Poems* (ed Peter Whiteford), Victoria University Press, Wellington, 1994.

Edmond, Lauris, *A Matter of Timing*, Auckland University Press, Auckland, 1996.
— *Catching it*, Oxford University Press, Auckland, 1983.
— *Seasons & Creatures*, Oxford University Press, Auckland, 1986.
— *Wellington Letter*, Mallinson Rendel, Wellington, 1980.

Edmond, Murray, *Letters & Paragraphs*, Caxton Press, Christchurch, 1987.

Eggleton, David, *Empty Orchestra*, Auckland University Press, Auckland, 1995.

Elworthy, David, *Landfall 31*, September 1954.

Ensing, Riemke, *Talking Pictures – Selected Poems*, HeadworX, Wellington, 2000.

Escott, Margaret, *Separation and/or Greeting*, Auckland University Press, Auckland, 1980.

Fairburn, A.R.D., *Selected Poems* (ed Mac Jackson), Victoria University Press, Wellington, 1995.

Faith, Rangi, *Unfinished Crossword*, Hazard Press, Christchurch, 1990.

Falconer, Alun, *War Poems and Lyrics*, Harry H. Tombs Ltd, Wellington, 1946.

Farrell, Fiona, *The Inhabited Initial*, Auckland University Press, Auckland, 1999.

Fawkes, Glenda, *A Talent for Flight*, Steele Roberts, Wellington, 1999.

Frame, Janet, *The Pocket Mirror*, Pegasus Press, Christchurch, 1967.

French, Anne, *All Cretans are Liars*, Auckland University Press, Auckland, 1987.
— *Cabin Fever*, Auckland University Press, Auckland, 1990.

Glover, Denis, *Enter Without Knocking*, Pegasus Press, Christchurch, 1971.

Grattan, Kathleen, *The Music of What Happens,* Writers and Artists Press, Auckland, 1987.

Gretton, H.W., *A Selection of Poems, Songs and Short Stories*, The Gisborne Herald, 1985.

Hall, Bernadette, *Still Talking*, Victoria University Press, Wellington, 1997.

Harlow, Michael, *Takahe 35*, 1998.
— *Vlaminck's Tie*, Auckland University Press/Oxford University Press, Auckland, 1985.

Hart-Smith, W., *Hand To Hand: A Garnering,* Butterfly Books, Springwood NSW, 1991.

Hawken, Dinah, *It has no sound and is blue*, Victoria University Press, Wellington, 1987.

Healey, Robin, *Night Kitchen*, Mallinson Rendel, Wellington, 1985.

Horrocks, Ingrid, *Natsukashii*, Pemmican Press, Wellington, 1998.

Hulme, Keri, *Strands,* Auckland University Press, Auckland, 1992.

Hunt, Sam, *Collected Poems*, Penguin, Auckland, 1980.

Hyde, Robin, *Houses by the Sea*, Caxton Press, Christchurch, 1952.
— *Persephone in Winter*, Hurst & Blackett, London, 1937.

Ireland, Kevin, *Anzac Day. Selected Poems*, Hazard Press, Christchurch, 1997.
— *Educating the Body*, Caxton Press, Christchurch, 1967.
— *The Dangers of Art*, Cicada Press, Auckland, 1980.

Jackaman, Rob, *Triptych*, Hazard Press, Christchurch, 1988.

Jackson, Michael, *Going On*, John McIndoe, Dunedin, 1985.

Jacobs, Helen, *The Usefulness of Singing*, Sudden Valley Press, Christchurch, 1999.

Jansen, Adrienne, *How Things Are*, Whitireia Publishing and Daphne Brasell Ass., Wellington, 1996.

Johnson, Louis, *Last Poems*, Antipodes Press, Plimmerton, 1990.
— *New Worlds for Old*, Capricorn Press, Wellington, 1957.
— *Winter Apples*, Mallinson Rendel, Wellington, 1984.

Johnson, Mike, *Treasure Hunt*, Auckland University Press, Auckland, 1996.

Johnston, Andrew, *The Sounds*, Victoria University Press, Wellington, 1996.

Joseph, M.K., *Inscription on a Paper Dart: Selected Poems 1945–72*, Auckland University Press/Oxford University Press, Auckland, 1974.

Kassabova, Kapka, *All roads lead to the sea*, Auckland University Press, Auckland, 1997.

Kemp, Jan, *Against the Softness of Woman*, Caveman Press, Dunedin, 1976.

Kidman, Fiona, *Wakeful Nights*, Vintage, Auckland, 1991.

Lambert, Leonard, *A Washday Romance*, John McIndoe, Dunedin, 1980.
— *Park Island*, John McIndoe, Dunedin, 1990.

Leggott, Michele *As far as I can see*, Auckland University Press, Auckland, 1999.

Lonie, Iain, *The Entrance to Purgatory*, John McIndoe, Dunedin, 1986.
— *Winter Walk at Morning*, Victoria University Press, Wellington, 1991.

McAlpine, Rachel, *Selected Poems*, Mallinson Rendel, Wellington, 1988.

MacKenzie, Joy, *Sport 20*, Autumn 1998.

Macpherson, Mary, *The Inland Eye*, Pemmican Press, Wellington, 1998.

McQueen, Cilla, *anti gravity*, John McIndoe, Dunedin, 1984.
— *Homing In*, John McIndoe, Dunedin, 1982.

McQueen, Harvey, *Pingandy: New & Selected Poems*, HeadworX, Wellington, 1999.

Manhire, Bill, *Good Looks*, Auckland University Press/Oxford University Press, Auckland, 1982.
— *How to Take Off Your Clothes at the Picnic*, Wai-te-ata Press, Wellington, 1977.
— *What to Call Your Child*, Godwit, Auckland, 1999.

Mansfield, Katherine, *Poems of Katherine Mansfield* (ed Vincent O'Sullivan), Oxford University Press, London, 1988.

Mason, R.A.K, *Collected Poems*, Victoria University Press, Wellington, 1990.

Minehan, Mike, *Embracing the Dark*, Hazard Press, Christchurch, 1991.

Mitcalfe, Barry (translator), *Maori Poetry: The Singing Word*, Price Milburn for Victoria University Press, Wellington, 1974.

Morrissey, Michael, *Landfall 167*, September 1988.

Nannestad, Elizabeth, *If He's A Good Dog He'll Swim*, Auckland University Press, Auckland, 1996.

Neale, Emma, *Sleeve-notes*, Godwit, Auckland, 1999.

Newton, John, *The Listener*, 16 November 1985.

Ngata, Sir Apirana, *Nga Moteatea*, Part 1, The Polynesian Society, 1959.

Norcliffe, James, *A Kind of Kingdom*, Victoria University Press, Wellington, 1998.
— *The Sportsman & Other Poems*, Hard Echo Press, Auckland, 1987.

O'Brien, Gregory, *Days Beside Water*, Auckland University Press, Auckland, 1993.
— *Winter I Was*, Victoria University Press, Wellington, 1999.

O'Connor, John, *A Particular Context*, Sudden Valley Press, Christchurch, 1999.

Oliver, W.H., *Out of Season*, Oxford University Press, Wellington, 1980.

Orr, Bob, *Breeze*, Auckland University Press, Auckland, 1991.

Orsman, Chris, *Ornamental Gorse*, Victoria University Press, Wellington, 1994.
— *South*, Victoria University Press, Wellington, 1996.

O'Sullivan, Vincent, *Seeing You Asked*, Victoria University Press, Wellington, 1998.
— *The Rose Ballroom and other Poems*, John McIndoe, Dunedin, 1982.

Paterson, Alistair, *Birds Flying*, Pegasus Press, Christchurch, 1973.

Pirie, Mark, *Shoot*, Sudden Valley Press, Christchurch, 1999.

Plumb, Vivienne, *Avalanche*, Pemmican Press, Wellington, 2000.
— *Salamanca*, HeadworX, Wellington 1998.

Potiki, Roma, *Shaking the Tree*, Steele Roberts, Wellington, 1998.

Quigley, Sarah, *Auckland University Press New Poets 1*, Auckland University Press, Auckland, 1999.

Ranger, Laura, *Laura's Poems*, Godwit, Auckland, 1995.

Riach, Alan, *First & Last Songs*, Auckland University Press, Auckland, 1995.

Ricketts, Harry, *Coming Here*, Nagare Press, Palmerston North, 1989.
— *How Things Are*, Whitireia Publishing and Daphne Brasell Ass., Wellington, 1996.

Roddick, Alan, *Poetry New Zealand II*, Pegasus Press, Christchurch, 1974.

Sewell, Bill, *El Sur*, Pemmican Press, Wellington, 1998.
— *Erebus. A poem*, Hazard Press, Christchurch, 1999.

Sinclair, Keith, *Moontalk*, Auckland University Press, Auckland, 1993.

Smither, Elizabeth, *The Lark Quartet*, Auckland University Press, Auckland, 1999.
— *The Tudor Style: Poems New and Selected*, Auckland University Press, Auckland, 1993.
— *You're Very Seductive William Carlos Williams*, John McIndoe, Dunedin, 1978.

Smithyman, Kendrick, *Selected Poems* (ed Peter Simpson), Auckland University Press, Auckland, 1989.

Spear, Charles, *Twopence Coloured*, Caxton Press, Christchurch, 1951.

Stace, Jeanette, *Landfall 125*, March 1978.

Stanley, Mary, *The Starveling Year and Other Poems*, Auckland University Press, Auckland, 1994.

Stead, C.K., *Quesada*, The Shed, Auckland, 1975.
— *Crossing the Bar*, Auckland University Press/Oxford University Press, Auckland, 1972.
— *Walking Westward*, The Shed, Auckland, 1979.

Sturm, J.C., *Dedications*, Steele Roberts, Wellington, 1996.

Sullivan, Robert, *Star Waka*, Auckland University Press, Auckland, 1999.

Taylor, Apirana, *Eyes of the Ruru*, Voice Press, Wellington, 1979.

Turner, Brian, *Ancestors*, John McIndoe, Dunedin, 1981.
— *Bones*, John McIndoe, Dunedin, 1985.

Tuwhare, Hone, *Mihi: Collected Poems*, Penguin, Auckland, 1987.

Varcoe, Rae, *New Zealand Books 30*, 1997.

Ward, Raymond, *Settler and Stranger*, Caxton Press, Christchurch, 1965.

Wedde, Ian, *Earthly: Sonnets for Carlos*, Amphedesma Press, Akaroa, 1975.
— *Georgicon*, Victoria University Press, Wellington, 1984.
— *The Drummer*, Auckland University Press, Auckland, 1993.

Wendt, Albert, *Shaman of Visions*, Auckland University Press/Oxford University Press, Auckland, 1984.

Were, Virginia, *Jump Start*, Victoria University Press, Wellington, 1999.

Weston, Tom, *The Ambiguous Companion*, Hazard Press, Christchurch, 1996.

Wilson, Patrick, *The Bright Sea*, Pegasus Press, Christchurch, 1950.

Witheford, Hubert, *A Blue Monkey for the Tomb*, Faber, London, 1994.
— *A Native, Perhaps Beautiful*, Caxton Press, Christchurch, 1967.

Wright, David McKee, *The Station Ballads & Other Verses*, John A. Lee, Auckland, 1945.

INDEX OF TITLES AND FIRST LINES

(Titles are in italics)